ANNE WILLAN'S
LOOK & COOK

Superb Salads

ANNE WILLAN'S
LOOK & COOK

Superb Salads

DORLING KINDERSLEY
LONDON • NEW YORK • STUTTGART

A DORLING KINDERSLEY BOOK

Created and Produced by
CARROLL & BROWN LIMITED
5 Lonsdale Road
London NW6 6RA

Editorial Director Jeni Wright
Editor Stella Vayne
Editorial Assistant Julia Alcock

Art Editor Lyndel Donaldson
Designer Alan Watt
Production Editor Wendy Rogers

First American Edition, 1993
10 9 8 7 6 5 4 3 2

Published in the United States by
Dorling Kindersley, Inc., 232 Madison Avenue
New York, New York 10016

Willan, Anne.
    Superb salads / by Anne Willan. – 1st American ed.
        p.   cm. – (Look and cook)
    Includes index.
    ISBN 1-56458-301-5
    1. Cookery, Salads.   I. Title: Superb Salads.
II. Series: Willan, Anne. Look and cook.
TX807.W556 1993
641.8'3 – dc20   93-21802
                                                                        CIP

Reproduced by Colourscan, Singapore
Printed and bound in Spain by Artes Gráficas Toledo, S.A.
D.L.TO:621-1994

CONTENTS

SALADS

THE LOOK & COOK APPROACH

Welcome to **Superb Salads** and the *Look & Cook* series. These volumes are designed to be the simplest, most informative cookbooks you'll ever own. They are the closest I can come to sharing my personal techniques for cooking my own favorite recipes without actually being with you in the kitchen.

EQUIPMENT

Equipment and ingredients often determine whether or not you can cook a particular dish, so *Look & Cook* sets out everything you need at the beginning of each recipe. You'll see at a glance how long a recipe takes to cook, how many servings it makes, what the finished dish looks like, and how much preparation can be done ahead. When you start to cook, you'll find the preparation and cooking are organized into steps that are easy to follow. Each stage has its own color coding and everything is shown in photographs with brief text to go with each step. You will never be in doubt as to what it is you are doing, why you are doing it, and how it should look.

INGREDIENTS

🍽 SERVES 4-6   🥣 WORK TIME 25-35 MINUTES   🍲 COOKING TIME 20-30 MINUTES

I've also included helpful hints and ideas under "Anne Says." These may suggest an alternative ingredient or piece of equipment, or explain a certain method, or add some advice on mastering a particular technique. Similarly, if there is a crucial stage in a recipe when things can go wrong, I've included some warnings called "Take Care."

Many of the photographs are annotated to pinpoint why certain pieces of equipment work best, and how food should look at the various stages of cooking. Because presentation is so important, a picture of the finished dish with serving suggestions is at the end of each recipe.

Thanks to all this information, you can't go wrong. I'll be with you every step of the way. So please come with me into the kitchen to look, cook, and enjoy some **Superb Salads.**

WHY SALADS?

*Defining "salad" is not an easy task. History recounts that
the first salad was probably made up of fresh greens with a sprinkling of
salt to heighten flavor. By modern standards, a salad can – and does – contain nearly
every ingredient imaginable. One distinguishing feature is the dressing, whether a blend
of oil with vinegar or lemon juice, or a more esoteric concoction, including nuts, poppy seeds,
or soy sauce. Salads offer the freedom to follow your tastes, combining favorite ingredients
with a variety of dressings to serve as a first course or a complete meal.*

RECIPE CHOICE

The salad recipes in this volume are just a sampling of the abundant possibilities you can choose from. Many salads make a good first course and I start with these, leading into more substantial recipes that are suitable as a main course. Seasonal availability is important, so always select a salad with the time of year and fresh local ingredients in mind.

FIRST COURSE SALADS

Creative Garden Salad: salad at its simple best; fresh garden greens tossed in an oil and vinegar dressing, adorned with edible flowers. *Leeks Vinaigrette:* in the French tradition, leeks are marinated in vinaigrette dressing and topped with colorful sieved egg yolk, chopped egg white, and parsley. *Asparagus Vinaigrette:* the fresh asparagus of late spring is coated in light vinaigrette. *Greek Salad:* a rustic, country salad of feta cheese, cucumbers, tomatoes, red onion, and bell peppers in a lively vinaigrette dressing. *Mozzarella Cheese and Plum Tomato Salad:* a favorite starter from Italy, combining slices of plum tomatoes and chewy mozzarella cheese, with a sprinkling of vinaigrette dressing and chopped basil. *Pear, Fennel, and Walnut Salad:* slices of pear and anise-flavored fennel bulb are sprinkled with a chunky Gorgonzola dressing and chopped walnuts. *Apple and Fennel Salad:* slices of crisp red apple are paired with fennel, and garnished with a creamy Roquefort dressing. *Red Bean, Corn, and Bell Pepper Salad:* a salad in Southwestern style, teaming red kidney beans with corn and a trio of diced bell peppers, all served in a fiery chili vinaigrette. *Red Bean, Corn, and Onion Salad:* sweet corn and red kidney beans are a natural pair in this spicy first-course idea. *Two-Bean Salad with Guacamole:* colorful vegetables mingle with white and red kidney beans.

Springtime Rice Salad: colors of springtime are echoed in this rice salad with smoked salmon and asparagus. *Rice Salad with Smoked Trout and Peas:* flakes of smoked trout and green peas add character to white rice in a vinaigrette dressing. *Wilted Spinach Salad:* fresh spinach leaves are wilted with crispy hot bacon and a pungent reduction of red wine vinegar. *Wilted Escarole Salad:* hot bacon dressing complements the slight bitterness of winter escarole, garnished with slices of Parmesan cheese. *Melon and Mint Salad:* a quick summer salad of melon, cherry tomatoes, and freshly chopped mint in a port wine and lemon dressing. *Melon and Cucumber Salad:* crisp cucumber and sweet grapes are good partners for melon in this cooling salad. *Tangy Melon Salad:* the addition of onion and orange makes a lively melon salad, good served with Mexican dishes or an Indian curry. *Black Forest Potato Salad:* Germanic flavors predominate in this potato salad with Westphalian ham and a dressing of sour cream with caraway seeds. *Yankee Potato Salad:* American picnic fare that is a harbinger of the backyard barbecue season. *Shrimp and Zucchini Salad with Saffron:* an Italian-style antipasto salad with butterflied jumbo shrimp marinated in saffron, then broiled, and served with zesty marinated zucchini. *Marinated Shrimp and Mushroom Salad:* marinated button mushrooms and broiled shrimp make a delectable appetizer. *Creamy Coleslaw:* a creamy vinaigrette dressing binds this traditional mix of shredded cabbage and grated carrot. *Apple and Pineapple Coleslaw:* tart green apples and pineapple in a tangy buttermilk dressing make for a spirited rendition of coleslaw. *Green and Red Cabbage Coleslaw:* a striking duo, red cabbage replaces the carrot in this coleslaw. *Classic Caesar Salad:* this salad plays on quality ingredients of romaine lettuce, anchovies, Parmesan cheese, and lemon, with whole fresh egg for the characteristic creamy finish. *Caesar Salad with Tomatoes and Asparagus:* sun-dried tomatoes replace anchovies in this updated Caesar salad, with the addition of asparagus and fresh tomatoes. *Avocado and Grapefruit Salad with Prosciutto:* a happy trio of textures and flavors, served on a bed of peppery arugula with a poppy-seed dressing. *Avocado and Grapefruit Salad with Smoked Salmon:* a satisfying first course that also doubles as a summer lunch. *Indonesian Salad:* a salad of carrots, cauliflower, and cucumbers, served on a bed of bean sprouts, highlighted with a spicy peanut sauce, and garnished with omelet curls. *Bird's Nest Salad with Peanut Sauce:* the bright colors of red cabbage and green beans combine with potatoes and bean sprouts. *Fantasia Salad with Cheese Wafers:* salad greens are tossed with a raspberry dressing and served with slices of fresh figs, and tangy blue-cheese wafers. *Roasted Red Bell Pepper and Artichoke Salad with Cheese Wafers:* the robust sunny flavors of Italy dominate here. *Middle Eastern Salads:* a salad of bulghur wheat, tomato, and plenty of mint, together with a yogurt and cucumber salad evoke the Middle East. *Mediterranean Salads with Couscous:* fresh herbs are key in a couscous salad with tomato and mint, and a tzatziki of grated cucumber, yogurt, and spices. *Autumn Vegetable Salad:* a combination of thin strips of celery root in mustard mayonnaise and grated carrots with raisins in vinaigrette dressing. *Piquant Beet and Celery Root Salads:* grated beets, tossed in a caraway-seed vinaigrette, team up with celery root strips coated with horseradish dressing.

MAIN COURSE SALADS

Marinated Steak Salad with Red Onions: marinated beef is broiled, then sliced to serve with mushrooms and broiled red onions on a bed of lettuce. *Asian Stir-Fried Beef Salad:* soy sauce adds Asian flair to thin strips of beef, garnished with lettuce, shiitake mushrooms, scallions, and a sprinkling of sesame seeds. *Pasta and Mussel Salad:* pasta salad is a delicious contemporary classic, crowned here with steamed mussels in an herb and lemon dressing. *Pasta and Scallop Salad:* lightly fried sea scallops are perfect in this pasta salad with spinach bows and a creamy herb dressing. *Lentil Salad with Knackwurst:* a robust, country salad, perfect in winter. *White Beans with Salami:* this Italian salad is delicious served warm or cold. *Asian Noodle Salad:* flavors of the Far East unite in a salad of shrimp, snow peas, fresh coriander, and a sprinkling of peanuts. *Thai Noodle Salad:* Lemon grass lends Thai character to this noodle salad with pork strips and a squeeze of lime. *Salade Niçoise:* the time-honored combination of tuna, green beans, potatoes, tomatoes, and olives from Nice, on the Mediterranean coast of France. *Broiled Fresh Tuna Salade Niçoise:* in this update, broiled fresh tuna tops the traditional vegetables. *Waldorf Chicken Salad:* poached chicken is added to the traditional Waldorf mix of apples, walnuts, and celery. *Tropical Chicken Salad:* papaya, mango, and melon give tropical flavor to this salad, dressed with yogurt and spices. *Warm Salmon, Orange, and Lamb's Lettuce Salad:* chopped hazelnuts and hazelnut oil add the distinctive touch to this multi-colored salad. *Warm Monkfish Salad with Horseradish:* horseradish dressing is the perfect foil for sautéed monkfish served on a bed of lamb's lettuce. *Lacquered Chicken Salad:* fresh ginger root gives Asian flavor to marinated chicken breasts, with lettuce, bean sprouts, and baby corn. *Teriyaki Chicken Salad:* a teriyaki marinade of soy sauce, rice wine, ginger, and garlic, is paired with chicken breasts. *Thanksgiving Wild Rice Salad:* traditional American foods feature in this salad of wild rice with pecans, cranberries, and smoked turkey breast. *Wild Rice Salad with Smoked Duck Breast:* wild rice acts as a foil for smoked duck breast with wild mushrooms and walnuts.

EQUIPMENT

Salads need
very little in the
way of special
equipment, but
a few basic
items are vital.
First priority is a
sharp chef's knife
for chopping, together with
a small vegetable knife and a
thin-bladed, flexible filleting knife
for cutting fish escalopes and wafer
thin slices of vegetables, such as cucumber.

A salad spinner is good to have on hand; it simplifies drying lettuce and leafy greens, but a dish towel also does the job. You will need a colander for draining blanched vegetables, boiled pasta, and potatoes, as well as a mesh strainer for puréeing berries or sieving cooked egg yolk. A wire whisk is needed in the preparation of dressings.

Other standard kitchen equipment often used includes a vegetable peeler, grater, citrus juicer, wooden spoons for stirring, and slotted spoons for lifting foods from liquid or fat. You will occasionally need a saucepan or a frying pan. The oven is seldom used, but some recipes require a broiler pan and rack or a baking sheet for toasting nuts.

In this volume, I show you the techniques of chopping and slicing ingredients by hand, so that you will become comfortable with these manual methods. A mandoline is a manual slicer that makes the job easier and ensures even slices. However, if you have a food processor with the appropriate attachments, it will speed up slicing vegetables, cutting julienne, or shredding cabbage when large amounts are involved.

You can use almost any bowl for tossing salad, provided it is not made of aluminum or enamel, which will react with the acid of a vinaigrette dressing. I prefer the traditional wide wooden bowl that allows plenty of room for tossing. After a while the salad bowl becomes impregnated with dressing and acquires a patina of its own. Salad servers are specifically designed for tossing ingredients in the bowl, but two ordinary wooden spoons can also be used.

INGREDIENTS

Given the broad definition of a salad nowadays, the possible ingredients are innumerable. Many of the recipes in this book feature traditional lettuces — Boston, red leaf, romaine, and greens, such as spinach and cabbage, while others use more "gourmet" newcomers, such as arugula, lamb's lettuce (mâche), and radicchio. Flavor is often heightened with fresh herbs, such as curly or flat-leaf parsley, chives, tarragon, basil, coriander, mint, and dill. They are usually chopped and added to the dressing, but occasionally mixed as whole leaves into the salad itself.

Other classic raw salad ingredients include tomatoes, cucumbers, bean sprouts, celery, onions, and avocados. Sweet bell peppers are used both raw and roasted, while fresh hot chili peppers add their distinctive heat to a few of the recipes. Root vegetables, such as potatoes and beets, should be boiled before a dressing is added, but carrots may appear either raw or cooked. A sizeable number of salad recipes are based on grains or legumes, such as lentils, wild or long-grain rice, dried beans, or pasta. Cheeses such as Parmesan, feta, and blue varieties give salty bite to salads, as do olives, anchovies, and bacon. Nuts – walnuts, hazelnuts, peanuts, pecans – add distinctive background crunch.

Citrus fruit, particularly lemons, provide a delicious acidity in many salads, and you will find a variety of other fruit used: fresh figs, raspberries, apples, mangoes, and melons are among them. Seafood, such as shrimp, salmon, monkfish, tuna, sea scallops, and mussels add substance to some salads, while chicken, beef, ham, and sausages are used for a more hearty flavor.

TECHNIQUES

A successful salad requires little or no technical cooking knowledge. In this book you will see how to prepare a wide variety of salad greens and herbs, as well as an assortment of vegetables, from asparagus to zucchini. You'll find instructions on how to trim, peel, chop, grate, and slice them. Some vegetables must be blanched by boiling in water to soften their texture and remove bitter flavors; some are sautéed or broiled, and often they are marinated in dressing before serving, partly to tenderize them, partly to add flavor. Methods used for cooking meats and seafood for salads are usually rapid, and include broiling, poaching, stir-frying, and sautéing. Among salad accompaniments, you will find techniques for making croûtons and crumbly cheese wafers.

As with other volumes in the *Look & Cook* series, we describe in detail the basic techniques that are commonly used in these recipes. You will see how to chop herbs; how to peel tomatoes; how to wash and dry salad greens; how to chop onions and shallots; how to core, seed, and dice bell peppers and fresh hot chili peppers; how to toast nuts; how to hard-boil and shell eggs; and how to peel and section citrus fruit; how to make vinaigrette dressing; how to make chicken stock and a bouquet garni; how to seed grapes; and how to peel and chop ginger and garlic.

CREATIVE GARDEN SALAD

¶O¶ SERVES 8   ☕ WORK TIME 15–30 MINUTES

EQUIPMENT

salad spinner †

chef's knife

small knife

whisk

bowls

chopping board

† dish towel can also be used

The wide range of garden greens available year-round is an invitation to create your own personal salad. Fresh herbs can accent the mix, with a sprinkling of edible flowers. A homemade vinaigrette dressing, featuring extra-virgin olive oil or a nut oil, with your choice of vinegar, is indispensable.

GETTING AHEAD

The vinaigrette dressing can be made up to 1 week in advance and kept in a sealed container. Prepare the salad greens up to 1 day in advance and keep them, wrapped in a damp dish towel, in the refrigerator. Toss the salad just before serving.

SHOPPING LIST

2	heads of Belgian endive, total weight about 5 oz
1	small head of curly endive, weighing about 10 oz
1	medium head of radicchio, weighing about 5 oz
4 oz	lamb's lettuce (mâche)
4 oz	arugula
5–7	sprigs of fresh basil
5–7	sprigs of fresh tarragon
1	small bunch of fresh chives, with flowers if possible
1	package of edible flowers (optional)
	For the vinaigrette dressing
¼ cup	red wine vinegar
	salt and pepper
2 tsp	Dijon-style mustard (optional)
¾ cup	extra-virgin olive oil

INGREDIENTS

edible flowers

curly endive

arugula

Belgian endive

Dijon-style mustard

basil

radicchio

lamb's lettuce

chives

tarragon

olive oil

red wine vinegar

ORDER OF WORK

1 PREPARE THE SALAD GREENS

2 PREPARE THE HERBS, MAKE THE DRESSING, AND FINISH THE SALAD

1 PREPARE THE SALAD GREENS

1 Using the small knife, cut out and discard the core from the base of each Belgian endive. Discard any withered leaves. Wipe Belgian endives with a damp paper towel.

Discard core of Belgian endive which can be bitter

2 Using the chef's knife, cut each head of endive into ½-inch diagonal slices. Put the slices in a large bowl.

3 Cut the root end from the curly endive and discard the tough outer leaves. Pull the leaves apart, wash, and dry them (see box, below). Add the curly endive to the Belgian endive in the bowl.

Curly endive belongs to same family as Belgian endive but is green because it grows above ground

---

HOW TO WASH AND DRY SALAD GREENS

Salad greens can be washed in advance, wrapped loosely in paper towels or a dish towel, and stored up to 1 day in the refrigerator.

1 Immerse salad greens in a sink full of cold water, to loosen grit and soil and help crisp the leaves, 15–30 minutes.

2 Agitate the leaves to loosen any remaining grit. Lift the leaves one by one out of the water, and rinse them under cold, running water to remove any remaining soil.

Rinse individual salad leaves under cold, running water

3 Tear large leaves with your hands into 2–3 pieces. Dry the leaves using a salad spinner, or by patting dry with a dish towel or paper towels.

! TAKE CARE !
Wet leaves dilute dressing and reduce crispness.

4 Discard any discolored or withered outer leaves from the radicchio. Cut away the root end. Separate the leaves, wash, and dry them (see box, page 11). Add the radicchio to the large bowl.

Dark green arugula contrasts with purple radicchio and pale green endive

Purple and white radicchio adds vibrant color to salad leaves

Profusion of fresh salad leaves is very appetizing

5 Pinch away any root ends from the lamb's lettuce, keeping the small bunches of leaves intact. Wash and dry the leaves (see box, page 11). Add the lamb's lettuce to the bowl.

6 Wash and dry the arugula (see box, page 11), discarding the tough stems. Add the leaves to the bowl of salad greens.

2 PREPARE THE HERBS, MAKE THE DRESSING, AND FINISH THE SALAD

1 Nip any basil and tarragon tips from the stems. Strip the tarragon and basil leaves from the stems. If they have flowers, cut the chives 2 inches below the flowers and set aside. Cut the remainder of the chives into 1-inch lengths. Prepare the vinaigrette dressing (see box, page 13).

Chive flowers are pretty and edible

Whole basil leaves are added to salad leaves

2 Just before serving, add the basil, tarragon, and chives to the bowl of salad leaves. Whisk the dressing and pour it over the salad.

3 Gently toss the salad: lift a portion of the greens and let them fall; turn the bowl slightly and repeat until the greens are evenly coated in vinaigrette dressing. Taste the leaves to be sure that the seasoning is well balanced.

Toss salad leaves very thoroughly with dressing so they are evenly coated

4 Carefully place any chive flowers with other edible flowers on top of the salad, arranging them as decoratively as possible.

🍽 **TO SERVE**
Serve the salad immediately, while the leaves and flowers are fresh and retain their vibrant colors.

Make certain flowers are non-toxic

EDIBLE FLOWERS

Some flowers are toxic, so eat only store-bought or known edible flowers, grown without the use of pesticides or other chemical sprays. Listed below are just a few edible flowers.

Pansy • Rose • Marigold
Cornflower • Viola
Borage • Honeysuckle
Nasturtium

HOW TO MAKE VINAIGRETTE DRESSING

The standard recipe for vinaigrette dressing follows the principle of 1 part vinegar to 3 parts oil, but these quantities can vary according to taste and the other ingredients that are used.

1 In a small bowl, whisk the vinegar with the salt, pepper, and mustard, if using.

2 Gradually whisk in the oil in a steady stream so the vinaigrette dressing emulsifies and thickens slightly. Taste the dressing for seasoning.

ANNE SAYS
"A base of oil, vinegar, mustard, salt, and pepper can be kept up to 1 week in a sealed container at room temperature; add flavorings just before use."

LEEKS VINAIGRETTE

🍽 SERVES 4–6 🥄 WORK TIME 15–20 MINUTES* 🍲 COOKING TIME 15–25 MINUTES

EQUIPMENT

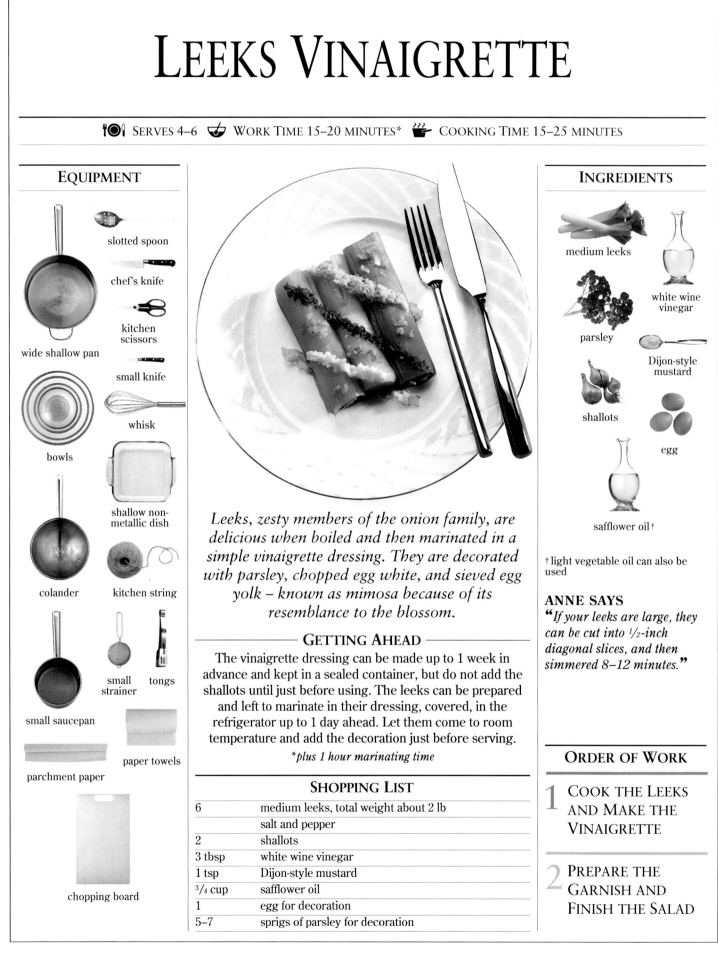

slotted spoon

chef's knife

kitchen scissors

wide shallow pan

small knife

whisk

bowls

shallow non-metallic dish

colander   kitchen string

small strainer   tongs

small saucepan

paper towels

parchment paper

chopping board

INGREDIENTS

medium leeks

white wine vinegar

parsley

Dijon-style mustard

shallots

egg

safflower oil †

† light vegetable oil can also be used

ANNE SAYS
"If your leeks are large, they can be cut into ½-inch diagonal slices, and then simmered 8–12 minutes."

Leeks, zesty members of the onion family, are delicious when boiled and then marinated in a simple vinaigrette dressing. They are decorated with parsley, chopped egg white, and sieved egg yolk – known as mimosa because of its resemblance to the blossom.

GETTING AHEAD

The vinaigrette dressing can be made up to 1 week in advance and kept in a sealed container, but do not add the shallots until just before using. The leeks can be prepared and left to marinate in their dressing, covered, in the refrigerator up to 1 day ahead. Let them come to room temperature and add the decoration just before serving.

*plus 1 hour marinating time

SHOPPING LIST

6	medium leeks, total weight about 2 lb
	salt and pepper
2	shallots
3 tbsp	white wine vinegar
1 tsp	Dijon-style mustard
¾ cup	safflower oil
1	egg for decoration
5–7	sprigs of parsley for decoration

ORDER OF WORK

1 COOK THE LEEKS AND MAKE THE VINAIGRETTE

2 PREPARE THE GARNISH AND FINISH THE SALAD

1 COOK THE LEEKS AND MAKE THE VINAIGRETTE

2 Wash each leek thoroughly, fanning it out under cold, running water, as leeks can be very gritty.

1 Trim the leeks, discarding the roots and tough green tops. Slit each one lengthwise in half, leaving the leeks attached at the root end.

Leeks tied with string keep their shape during cooking

Tie leeks into bundles for easy handling

3 Divide the leeks into 2 bundles, then tie them together at each end, using the kitchen string.

4 Fill the wide shallow pan with salted water and bring to a boil. Add the leeks, and simmer until tender, 15–25 minutes, depending on size.

ANNE SAYS
"A heatproof plate can be placed on top of the leeks to keep them submerged in water. You may need to add more water during cooking."

5 Meanwhile, prepare the vinaigrette dressing. Peel and chop the shallots (see box, page 16). In a bowl, whisk together the vinegar, mustard, salt, and pepper. Gradually whisk in the oil so the vinaigrette emulsifies and thickens slightly. Whisk in the shallots; taste for seasoning.

HOW TO CHOP A SHALLOT

For a standard chop, make slices that are about ⅛-inch thick. For a fine chop, make the slices as thin as possible.

1 Peel the outer, papery skin from the shallot. If necessary, separate the shallot into sections at the root and peel the sections. Set the shallot or section on a chopping board, hold it steady with your fingers and slice horizontally toward the root, leaving the slices attached at the root end.

2 Slice vertically through the shallot, again leaving the root end uncut.

3 Cut across the shallot to make fine dice. Continue chopping, if necessary, until dice are very fine.

Rinse leeks with cold water to stop cooking process and help retain color

6 Test whether the leeks are tender by piercing with the tip of the small knife. Drain the leeks in the colander, rinse with cold water, and drain on paper towels.

7 Cut the leeks into 2- to 3-inch lengths for serving. Cut and discard the string.

Cut leeks in 2 or 3 lengths depending on size

8 Lay the leeks in the shallow dish. Briskly whisk the vinaigrette dressing and pour it over the leeks. Cover, and leave the leeks to marinate in the refrigerator, at least 1 hour.

2 PREPARE THE GARNISH AND FINISH THE SALAD

1 Take the marinated leeks from the refrigerator and let them come to room temperature. Hard-boil and shell the egg. Cut the egg in half, then separate the yolk from the white with your fingers.

2 Coarsely chop the white. Put the yolk in the small strainer set over a bowl. Work the yolk through, using the back of a spoon. Scrape away the yolk clinging to the bottom of the strainer.

3 Divide the leeks between 4–6 individual plates. Strip the parsley leaves from the stems and pile the leaves on the chopping board. Finely chop them. Spread the parsley on a sheet of parchment paper. Scoop a line of parsley onto the edge of the chef's knife blade.

4 Holding the blade at a diagonal on top of the leeks, gently tap it so the parsley drops in a neat line onto them. Repeat the process of spreading on paper, scooping onto the knife, and tapping over the leeks with the egg white and egg yolk. Serve immediately, at room temperature.

Egg yolk makes pretty mimosa garnish

Cooked and marinated leeks are tender and tasty

V A R I A T I O N
ASPARAGUS VINAIGRETTE
Fresh green asparagus is a delectable replacement for leeks in this vinaigrette salad. It can be served warm or at room temperature.

1 Prepare the vinaigrette dressing as directed in the main recipe, using sherry vinegar in place of the white wine vinegar.

2 Omit the leeks. Trim 2 lb asparagus spears. If necessary strip away tough outer skin from the asparagus stems, and trim off woody ends. Tie the asparagus into 4–6 bundles with kitchen string for easy handling. Bring a large saucepan of salted water to a boil, and simmer the asparagus just until tender when pierced with a knife, 5–7 minutes. Drain the asparagus, rinse with cold water, and drain again thoroughly.

3 Omit the parsley. Marinate and finish the salad as directed, decorating with criss-cross lines of egg white and egg yolk.

GREEK SALAD

EQUIPMENT

bowls

vegetable peeler

small knife

chef's knife

large metal spoon

whisk

chopping board

Salty feta cheese, pungent black olives, and fragrant olive oil are key elements in any Greek kitchen. Here they are combined with tomatoes, onion, bell peppers, and crisp cucumbers – a refreshing combination found throughout Greece.

GETTING AHEAD

The salad ingredients can be prepared up to 6 hours ahead and refrigerated. The vinaigrette dressing can be made 1 week in advance and kept in a sealed container. Whisk the dressing to re-emulsify it and add the herbs just before using. Toss the salad about 30 minutes before serving.

*plus 30 minutes standing time

SHOPPING LIST

2 lb	medium tomatoes
2	medium cucumbers
2	green bell peppers
1	medium red onion
6 oz	feta cheese
3/4 cup	Kalamata or other Greek olives
	For the herb vinaigrette dressing
3–5	sprigs of fresh mint
3–5	sprigs of fresh oregano
7–10	sprigs of parsley
3 tbsp	red wine vinegar
	salt and pepper
1/2 cup	extra-virgin olive oil

INGREDIENTS

tomatoes

cucumbers

parsley

red onion

feta cheese

olive oil

bell peppers

oregano

mint

red wine vinegar

olives

ANNE SAYS
"*The fruitiness of extra-virgin olive oil will make a great difference to this recipe.*"

ORDER OF WORK

1 **MAKE THE HERB VINAIGRETTE DRESSING**

2 **PREPARE THE VEGETABLES**

3 **CUBE THE CHEESE AND ASSEMBLE THE SALAD**

1 MAKE THE HERB VINAIGRETTE DRESSING

1 Strip the mint and oregano leaves from the stems and pile them together on the chopping board.

2 Coarsely chop the leaves, bunching them together with one hand to make chopping easier. Strip the parsley leaves from the stems and chop them.

Mint is distinctive ingredient in herb vinaigrette dressing

3 In a small bowl, whisk together the red wine vinegar, salt, and pepper. Gradually whisk in the oil so the vinaigrette dressing emulsifies and thickens slightly.

4 Add the chopped herbs, then whisk the dressing again and taste for seasoning.

Fresh herbs contribute fragrance and flavor

2 PREPARE THE VEGETABLES

Always use the ripest tomatoes you can find

Halved tomato wedges are bite-sized and will mingle colorfully with other ingredients

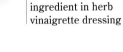

1 With the tip of the small knife, core the tomatoes. Cut each one into 8 wedges, then cut each wedge in half.

Vegetable peeler avoids wastage

2 With the vegetable peeler, peel the cucumbers. Trim and cut each cucumber lengthwise in half.

3 Scoop out the seeds from each cucumber half with a teaspoon. Discard the seeds.

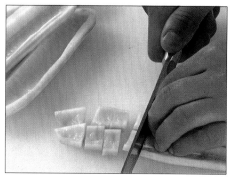

4 Cut the cucumber halves lengthwise into 2–3 strips, then gather the strips together and cut them crosswise into ½-inch pieces.

Dicing with chef's knife is quick and efficient

5 Cut around, pull out, and discard each bell pepper core. Halve the peppers, scrape out the seeds, and cut away the white ribs. Set each half cut-side down, flatten it with the heel of your hand, and slice it lengthwise into strips. Cut the strips into dice.

6 Peel and trim the red onion. Cut a thin slice from one side so it sits firmly on the chopping board. Cut the onion crosswise into thin rings. Separate the rings with your fingers.

3 CUBE THE CHEESE AND ASSEMBLE THE SALAD

1 Cut the feta cheese into ½-inch strips. Gather the strips together and cut crosswise into cubes.

2 Put the tomatoes, cucumbers, bell peppers, and onion rings in a large bowl. Briskly whisk the herb vinaigrette dressing and pour it over the top of the salad.

Vinaigrette dressing is fragrant with chopped, fresh herbs

3 With the large metal spoon, toss the vegetables thoroughly in the herb vinaigrette dressing.

Cubes of feta cheese give Greek salad characteristic flavor

4 Add the olives and feta cheese to the vegetables and gently toss again. Taste the salad for seasoning.

ANNE SAYS
"In Greece, olives would be left whole for the salad, but you may prefer to pit them, using an olive pitter."

Black olives
are essential
ingredient

🍽 TO SERVE
Allow the flavors to mellow before serving, about 30 minutes.

Feta cheese cubes
give substance to
lighter ingredients

Onion rings
add zing to salad

V A R I A T I O N

MOZZARELLA CHEESE AND PLUM TOMATO SALAD

1 Omit the bell peppers, onion, and feta cheese. Cut 1 lb mozzarella cheese into thin slices. Core 6 plum tomatoes, and cut each one crosswise into 6 slices. Peel, halve, and seed 1 cucumber. Cut each half into 6 lengthwise strips, then gather the strips into a bundle and cut them into 1/4-inch dice.

2 Chop 2 garlic cloves: set the flat side of a chef's knife on top of each garlic clove and strike it with your fist to lightly crush it. Discard the skin and finely chop the garlic.

3 Strip the leaves from the stems of 1 small bunch of fresh basil, and coarsely chop them in place of the mint, oregano, and parsley, reserving some basil leaves for garnish, if you like.

4 Make the vinaigrette dressing as directed in the main recipe, whisking in the chopped garlic with the chopped basil, and taste for seasoning.

5 Arrange alternating slices of mozzarella and plum tomatoes on individual plates. Set the cucumbers in a small cluster in the center of each serving. Briskly whisk the vinaigrette dressing and spoon it over the salad. Garnish with the reserved basil leaves.

PEAR, FENNEL, AND WALNUT SALAD

🍽️ SERVES 6 🥣 WORK TIME 30–35 MINUTES

EQUIPMENT

whisk

melon baller †

vegetable peeler

baking sheet

bowl

chef's knife

thin-bladed knife

small knife

metal spoon

chopping board

† teaspoon can also be used

Gorgonzola dressing adds an Italian touch to this salad of sliced ripe pears and fennel, and crunchy, toasted walnuts. The piquancy of the dressing contrasts well with the sweetness of the dessert pears and the aniseed flavor of the fennel.

GETTING AHEAD

You can make the Gorgonzola dressing and toast the walnuts up to 1 day ahead. Refrigerate the dressing and keep the nuts in sealed containers. Slice the pears and fennel and finish the salad not more than 30 minutes before serving.

SHOPPING LIST

½ cup	walnut pieces
1	large fennel bulb, weighing about ¾ lb
3	ripe Comice or other dessert pears, total weight about 1¼ lb
1	lemon
	For the Gorgonzola dressing
4 oz	Gorgonzola cheese
¼ cup	red wine vinegar
	salt and pepper
⅓ cup	olive oil

INGREDIENTS

dessert pears   fennel

lemon   walnuts

olive oil   red wine vinegar

Gorgonzola cheese

ANNE SAYS

"When selecting blue cheese, check that the rind is firm but not cracked, moist but not soggy. The cheese should have a piquant smell, and should be creamy, and well marbled with blue."

ORDER OF WORK

1 TOAST THE WALNUTS AND MAKE THE DRESSING

2 PREPARE AND ASSEMBLE THE SALAD

1 TOAST THE WALNUTS AND MAKE THE DRESSING

1 Heat the oven to 350°F. Spread the walnuts on the baking sheet and toast them in the heated oven until crisp, stirring occasionally so they color evenly, 5–8 minutes.

Zesty flavor is partly produced by marbling of blue veins in cheese

Firm Gorgonzola cheese is easily crumbled with your fingers

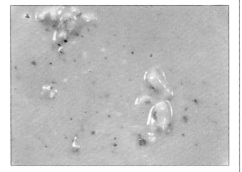

2 Meanwhile, cut the rind from the Gorgonzola and crumble the cheese with your fingers. If it is very soft, crush it with the tines of a fork.

3 Put two-thirds of the Gorgonzola cheese in the bowl with the red wine vinegar, salt, and pepper, and whisk together until mixed.

Dressing is thickened with cheese so it emulsifies when oil is whisked in

4 Gradually whisk in the oil so the Gorgonzola dressing emulsifies and thickens slightly. Stir the remaining crumbled cheese into the dressing, so a few larger pieces are left intact, and taste for seasoning. Cover the dressing and chill in the refrigerator while preparing the salad.

2 PREPARE AND ASSEMBLE THE SALAD

1 Trim the stems, root end, and any tough outer pieces from the fennel. Reserve any fronds for decoration. Cut the fennel bulb lengthwise in half.

2 Set each fennel half flat-side down on the chopping board and slice it lengthwise.

3 Peel the pears with the vegetable peeler, then cut out the flower and stem ends with the small knife.

Pears should be firm but ripe

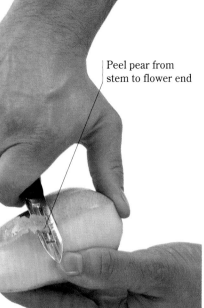

Peel pear from stem to flower end

4 Halve the pears lengthwise and scoop out the core from each half with the melon baller.

ANNE SAYS
"You can also use a teaspoon or small knife to remove the pear cores."

Lemon juice preserves color of pear slices

5 Set a pear half cut-side down and cut it lengthwise into thin slices, using the thin-bladed knife. Cut the lemon in half and squeeze lemon juice over the pear slices.

6 Continue slicing pear halves, squeezing lemon juice over each pear half after slicing.

! TAKE CARE !
Be sure that the pear slices are well coated in lemon juice so that they do not discolor.

Lengthwise pear slices are attractive for arranging on plates for serving

Spoon dressing over pears and fennel to lightly coat them

7 On individual plates, alternate the pear and fennel slices so that they overlap in a radiating pattern. Spoon on the Gorgonzola dressing.

🍴 TO SERVE

Scatter some toasted walnuts over each serving, and decorate with fennel fronds, if reserved.

Walnuts complement texture of pear and fennel slices

Gorgonzola is main flavoring ingredient in dressing

APPLE AND FENNEL SALAD

Crisp red-skinned apples, such as McIntosh or Red Delicious, feature in this variation on Pear, Fennel, and Walnut Salad. Slices of fennel are tossed with creamy Roquefort dressing and set on a bed of apple rings and lettuce.

1 Omit the walnut pieces, Gorgonzola dressing, and pears. Make the dressing: discard the rind from 4 oz Roquefort cheese and cut it into chunks. In a food processor or blender, combine the cheese and 2 tbsp white wine vinegar; work until smooth. Add 3/4 cup heavy cream and continue working just until combined. Do not overwork the dressing or it may curdle.

2 Cut off and discard the root end from 1 head of Boston lettuce. Separate and wash the leaves in plenty of cold water, discarding the tough stems. Dry the lettuce in a salad spinner or on a dish towel.

3 Trim and slice the fennel bulb as directed in the main recipe, reserving any fronds. Toss the fennel slices in the dressing and taste for seasoning.

4 Core 3 apples with an apple corer. Cut a thin slice from 1 side of each apple so the apples sit firmly on the chopping board, and cut them crosswise into 1/4-inch rings. Sprinkle the apple rings with lemon juice and toss to coat thoroughly.

5 To finish, arrange the lettuce leaves on 6 individual plates, breaking the central ribs so the leaves lie flat. Set the apple rings in an overlapping circle on the lettuce leaves and arrange the dressed fennel slices in the center of each serving.

Fennel fronds add touch of color to this first course salad

Red Bean, Corn, and Bell Pepper Salad

🍴 Serves 6–8 🥣 Work Time 25–30 minutes* 🍲 Cooking Time 1–1½ hours

Equipment

flameproof casserole

colander

saucepans

chef's knife

tongs

small knife

2-pronged fork

pastry brush

chopping board

slotted spoon

rubber gloves

whisk

bowls

baking sheet

kitchen string

Red beans with a confetti of bell peppers and yellow corn are the basis for this Tex-Mex salad. To vary the color, you could use white kidney beans or, even better, black-eyed peas. A piquant chili pepper vinaigrette dressing adds the characteristic finishing touch.

*plus 8 hours soaking time and 1 hour chilling time

Ingredients

bell peppers

red kidney beans

corn tortillas

hot green chili peppers

cider vinegar

cayenne pepper

tomatoes

fresh corn

onion

safflower oil

whole cloves

ground cumin

bouquet garni

fresh coriander

Shopping List

2 cups	dried red kidney beans
1	onion
2	whole cloves
1	bouquet garni made with 5–6 parsley stems, 2–3 sprigs of fresh thyme, and 1 bay leaf
	pepper and salt
4	ears of fresh corn
1	red bell pepper
1	green bell pepper
1	yellow bell pepper
1½ lb	tomatoes
6	corn tortillas
¼ tsp	cayenne pepper
	For the chili pepper vinaigrette dressing
1	small bunch of fresh coriander (cilantro)
½ cup	cider vinegar
½ tsp	ground cumin
3	fresh hot green chili peppers
½ cup	safflower oil, more for tortillas and baking sheet

Order of Work

1 **Prepare the Beans**

2 **Make the Chili Pepper Dressing**

3 **Prepare the Vegetables and Toss the Salad**

4 **Broil the Tortilla Strips; Finish the Salad**

PREPARE THE BEANS

1 Put the dried beans in a large bowl. Add water to cover generously and leave them to soak, at least 8 hours.

ANNE SAYS
"*As an alternative to soaking the beans, put them in a saucepan, and add water to cover. Bring to a boil and let simmer, 30 minutes. Drain the beans, rinse with cold water, and drain again.*"

2 Drain the beans, rinse with cold water, then drain the beans again thoroughly.

Clove-studded onion adds flavor to beans

Add generous amounts of water when starting to cook beans

Bouquet garni is tied to casserole handle for easy removal

3 Peel the onion and stud with the cloves. Put the beans in the casserole. Add the bouquet garni, onion, and pepper. Cover generously with water. Bring to a boil and boil 10 minutes, cover, and simmer until the beans are tender, 1–1½ hours, adding salt only halfway through cooking.

4 Lift a few beans from the casserole, let cool slightly, then pinch a bean between your finger and thumb; it should be very soft.

5 Drain the beans, discarding the onion and bouquet garni. Rinse the beans under cold, running water, and drain again thoroughly.

2 MAKE THE CHILI PEPPER DRESSING

2 Cut the chili peppers lengthwise in half, discarding the cores. Scrape out the seeds and cut away the fleshy white ribs. Cut each half into very thin strips, gather the strips together, and cut across into fine dice.

Wear rubber gloves when preparing fresh chili peppers as they can burn your skin

1 Strip the coriander leaves from the stems. Pile the leaves on the chopping board, and finely chop them with the chef's knife. Whisk together the vinegar, cumin, salt, and pepper.

3 Add the diced chili peppers to the whisked dressing ingredients.

ANNE SAYS
"Protect your hands with rubber gloves until you have finished dealing with fresh hot chili peppers."

4 Gradually whisk in the safflower oil so that the vinaigrette emulsifies and thickens slightly. Stir in the coriander, reserving a little for garnish; taste for seasoning.

3 PREPARE THE VEGETABLES AND TOSS THE SALAD

1 Remove the husks and silks from the ears of fresh corn. Bring a large saucepan of water to a boil, add the ears, and cook, 5–7 minutes.

ANNE SAYS
"If fresh corn is not available, substitute 2 cups defrosted corn kernels. Add them to the salad without cooking."

Be sure to discard all husks and silks from corn cob

2 Lift an ear of corn out of the saucepan: the corn is cooked if the kernels pop out easily when tested with the point of the small knife.

3 Drain the corn, let cool a little, and cut the kernels from the cob. Core and seed the red, green, and yellow bell peppers, and cut them into dice (see box, below).

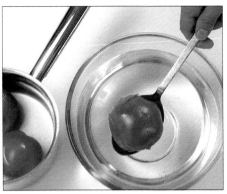

4 Core the tomatoes and score an "x" on the base of each. Immerse in boiling water until the skins start to split. Transfer to cold water.

Diced bell peppers are colorful salad ingredients

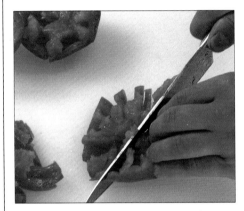

5 Peel the tomatoes, then cut each one crosswise in half; squeeze out the seeds, and coarsely chop each half.

Red kidney beans are plump and tender

6 In a large bowl, combine the red kidney beans, corn kernels, tomatoes, bell peppers, and chili pepper vinaigrette. Gently toss the salad and taste for seasoning. Cover, and chill in the refrigerator, at least 1 hour.

HOW TO CORE AND SEED A BELL PEPPER, AND CUT IT INTO STRIPS OR DICE

Before cutting a bell pepper into strips or dice, the core and seeds must be discarded.

1 With a small knife, cut around the bell pepper core. Twist the core, pull it out, and discard it. Halve the pepper lengthwise and scrape out the seeds. Cut away the white ribs on the inside of the pepper. Set each pepper half cut-side down on a work surface and press down on the top of the pepper half, with the heel of your hand, to flatten it for easier slicing.

Hold pepper firmly in palm of hand while coring

2 Using a chef's knife, slice each of the bell pepper halves lengthwise into thin strips.

3 For dice, gather the strips together and cut crosswise according to the size of dice required.

4 BROIL THE TORTILLA STRIPS; FINISH THE SALAD

1 Just before serving, heat the broiler and brush the baking sheet with oil. Brush the tortillas with oil, and season with salt and cayenne pepper.

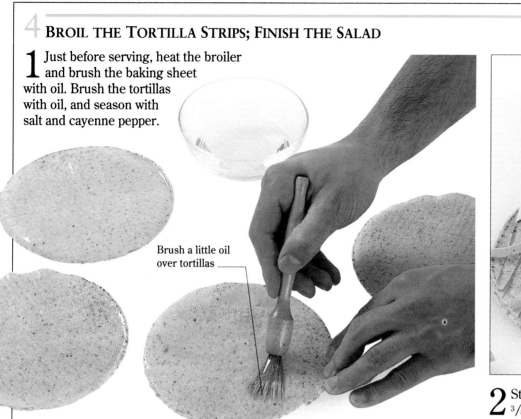

Brush a little oil over tortillas

2 Stack 3 tortillas and slice them into ³/₈-inch strips. Repeat with the remaining tortillas.

Toasted tortilla strips add crispness to salad

3 Spread the tortilla strips on the baking sheet. Broil, 4 inches from heat, until golden brown and crisp, stirring occasionally so the tortilla strips color evenly, 4–6 minutes.

🍽 TO SERVE
Divide the salad among 6–8 deep plates, and top each salad with tortilla strips. Sprinkle the reserved chopped coriander over the top, if you like. Serve chilled or at room temperature.

—— GETTING AHEAD ——
The salad can be made up to 2 days ahead and the flavor will mellow. Keep, covered, in the refrigerator. Prepare the tortilla strips just before serving.

V A R I A T I O N
RED BEAN, CORN, AND ONION SALAD

In this recipe, red onion and scallions replace the bell peppers. The salad is completed with crispy tortilla triangles.

1 Omit the bell peppers. Prepare the red kidney beans, corn, and tomatoes as directed. Make the chili pepper vinaigrette dressing as directed.

2 Peel 1 large red onion, leaving a little of the root attached, and cut it lengthwise in half. Lay each onion half flat on a chopping board and slice horizontally toward the root, leaving the slices attached at the root end, and then slice vertically, again leaving the root end uncut. Finally, cut across the onion to make dice.

3 With a chef's knife, trim and thinly slice 2 scallions, including some of their green tops.

4 Assemble the salad as directed, cover, and chill in the refrigerator, at least 1 hour.

5 Meanwhile, heat the broiler. Grate 3 oz Monterey Jack cheese. Arrange 6 corn tortillas on a baking sheet. Brush them with 1 tbsp oil and broil until crisp, 2–3 minutes. Remove the tortillas from the heat and sprinkle with the grated cheese, cayenne pepper, and salt. Return them to the heat and broil until the cheese is melted, 1–2 minutes longer. Transfer the tortillas to a chopping board and cut each one into 6 triangles.

6 Spoon the salad onto a large serving plate, and garnish with coriander leaves, if you like. Serve the crispy tortilla triangles separately.

V A R I A T I O N
TWO-BEAN SALAD WITH GUACAMOLE

In this colorful variation on a theme, red and white kidney beans are mixed with chili pepper vinaigrette dressing while they are still hot. Make the guacamole, and add the bell peppers, tomatoes, and scallions shortly before serving the salad.

1 Omit the corn and yellow bell pepper. Soak ³/₄ cup dried red kidney beans as directed. Soak separately ³/₄ cup dried white kidney beans. Prepare 2 clove-studded onions and 2 bouquets garnis. Cook the beans as directed, using 2 separate saucepans. Drain the beans, discard the clove-studded onions and bouquets garnis, and rinse the beans in hot water. Drain again, and transfer to a bowl.

2 Meanwhile, make the chili pepper vinaigrette dressing as directed. While the beans are still hot, pour the dressing over them, and stir to mix well. Let cool.

3 Meanwhile, prepare the green and red bell peppers and the tomatoes as directed. Make the guacamole: peel and chop 1 garlic clove and place in a bowl. Cut lengthwise around the center of each of 3 avocados (total weight 1¹/₂ lb) to the pit. Twist to loosen the halves and pull them apart. With a chopping movement, embed the blade of a chef's knife in the pit, and lift it free. Scrape the avocado pulp into the bowl. Combine the avocado and garlic with a fork, mashing the avocado against the side of the bowl. Add a pinch of salt and 4–5 drops of Tabasco sauce. Add the juice of 1 lime and stir the guacamole well to mix.

4 Assemble the salad: arrange a ring of beans on each of 6–8 plates. Spoon the guacamole in the center of the beans. Decorate with coriander sprigs, if you like.

SPRINGTIME RICE SALAD

🍴 SERVES 4–6 🥄 WORK TIME 20–25 MINUTES* 🍲 COOKING TIME 15–20 MINUTES

EQUIPMENT

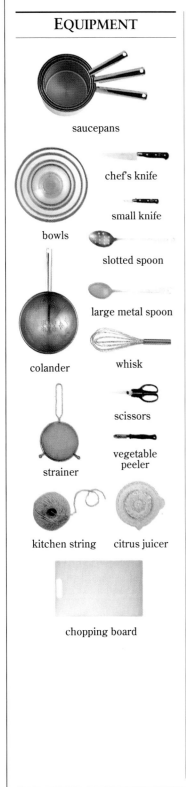

saucepans

chef's knife

small knife

bowls

slotted spoon

large metal spoon

colander

whisk

scissors

strainer

vegetable peeler

kitchen string

citrus juicer

chopping board

Spring flavors and colors are combined in a salad of green asparagus, pink smoked salmon, and fluffy white rice. The sweet, herb flavor of tarragon comes through discreetly in the tarragon vinegar of the dressing. You can make your own flavored vinegars at home, or use a commercially prepared herb vinegar.

GETTING AHEAD

The vinaigrette dressing can be made up to 1 week in advance and kept in a sealed container. The rice salad can be made up to 1 day in advance and kept, covered, in the refrigerator. Let the salad come to room temperature before serving.

*plus 1 hour chilling time

SHOPPING LIST

1	lemon
1 cup	long-grain rice
1/2 lb	asparagus
3	celery stalks
1/2 lb	sliced smoked salmon
	salt and pepper
	For the vinaigrette dressing
3 tbsp	tarragon vinegar
2 tsp	Dijon-style mustard
3/4 cup	safflower oil

INGREDIENTS

smoked salmon

long-grain rice

asparagus

safflower oil †

celery stalks

lemon

tarragon vinegar

Dijon-style mustard

† light vegetable oil can also be used

ANNE SAYS

"If the asparagus is young and the stems slender, the stems will not need peeling before cooking."

ORDER OF WORK

1 COOK THE RICE AND MAKE THE VINAIGRETTE DRESSING

2 PREPARE THE VEGETABLES AND SALMON; ASSEMBLE THE SALAD

1 COOK THE RICE AND MAKE THE VINAIGRETTE DRESSING

1 Bring a large saucepan of salted water to a boil. Squeeze the juice from half of the lemon into the water, then add the lemon half to the water.

2 Add the rice to the water, stir, and bring back to a fast boil. Simmer until the rice is just tender, stirring occasionally while the rice is cooking, 10–12 minutes.

3 Meanwhile, make the vinaigrette dressing. Put the vinegar, salt, and pepper in a small bowl. Add the mustard, and whisk together.

Lemon adds flavor and bleaches rice

Add rice slowly so water continues to boil

Pour oil in slow, steady stream when making vinaigrette dressing

4 Gradually whisk in the oil so the vinaigrette emulsifies and thickens slightly. Taste the vinaigrette dressing for seasoning and set aside.

5 Drain the rice, discard the lemon half, then rinse with cold water to wash away the starch, and drain again thoroughly. Transfer the rice to a large bowl. Squeeze and reserve the juice from the remaining lemon half.

2 PREPARE THE VEGETABLES AND SALMON; ASSEMBLE THE SALAD

1 With the vegetable peeler, strip away the tough outer skin from the asparagus stems, and trim off the woody ends.

Vegetable peeler removes skin quickly and easily

Prepare asparagus just before cooking because it dries out quickly

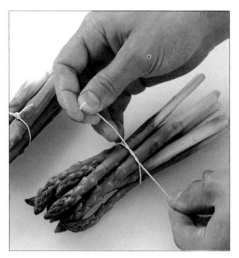

2 Tie the asparagus stems in 2 equal bundles with kitchen string for easy handling.

3 Bring a large saucepan of salted water to a boil, add the asparagus, and simmer just until tender when pierced with the tip of the small knife, 5–7 minutes.

4 Drain the asparagus, rinse under cold, running water, and drain again thoroughly. Discard the strings. Trim off about 2 inches of the asparagus tips and reserve them. Cut the stems into 1/2-inch pieces.

5 Peel the strings from the celery stalks with the vegetable peeler. Cut each stalk crosswise into 3-inch long pieces, then cut each piece lengthwise into 2–3 strips. Stack the strips and cut across to make small dice.

Smoked salmon slices need not be wafer thin

Curl fingers under when slicing salmon into strips

6 With the chef's knife, cut the smoked salmon slices crosswise into 1/2-inch strips.

7 Briskly whisk the vinaigrette to re-emulsify it and pour it over the rice, reserving 1–2 tbsp.

8 Add the chopped asparagus, celery, smoked salmon, and reserved lemon juice to the rice and vinaigrette dressing.

Smoked salmon completes this delicately flavored salad

9 Toss the ingredients together until mixed, and taste the salad for seasoning. Cover, and chill in the refrigerator, at least 1 hour. Before serving, let come to room temperature.

🍴 TO SERVE
Serve in bowls, decorated with asparagus tips brushed with reserved dressing.

Asparagus tips are a tender and distinctive garnish

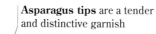

Smoked salmon is delicious dressed with vinaigrette

VARIATION

RICE SALAD WITH SMOKED TROUT AND PEAS

The vivid green of peas and red of tomatoes add color to smoked trout and rice.

1 Omit the smoked salmon and the asparagus. Cook the rice and make the vinaigrette dressing as directed.

2 Bring a small saucepan of salted water to a boil, add 1 cup shelled, fresh green peas, and simmer just until tender, 3–5 minutes. Drain, rinse with cold water, and drain again thoroughly. Alternatively, use the same quantity of frozen green peas, cooked according to package directions.

3 Using a small knife, peel the skin from 2 smoked trout (weighing about 1/2 lb each) and lift off the fillets, discarding the bones. Flake the flesh of the smoked trout with a fork.

4 Rinse 3/4 lb cherry tomatoes and dry them on paper towels. Discard the stems and cut 2 or 3 in half. Reserve the tomatoes for garnish.

5 Assemble the salad as directed and taste for seasoning. Transfer to a serving bowl and arrange the whole tomatoes around the edge and the halves in the center.

WILTED SPINACH SALAD

Salade Lyonnaise

🍽 SERVES 6   🥣 WORK TIME 30–35 MINUTES   🍲 COOKING TIME 20–25 MINUTES

EQUIPMENT

chef's knife

small knife

pastry brush

small saucepan

bowls

frying pan

strainer

wooden spoons

bread knife

metal spoon

baking sheet

dish towel †

chopping board

† salad spinner can also be used

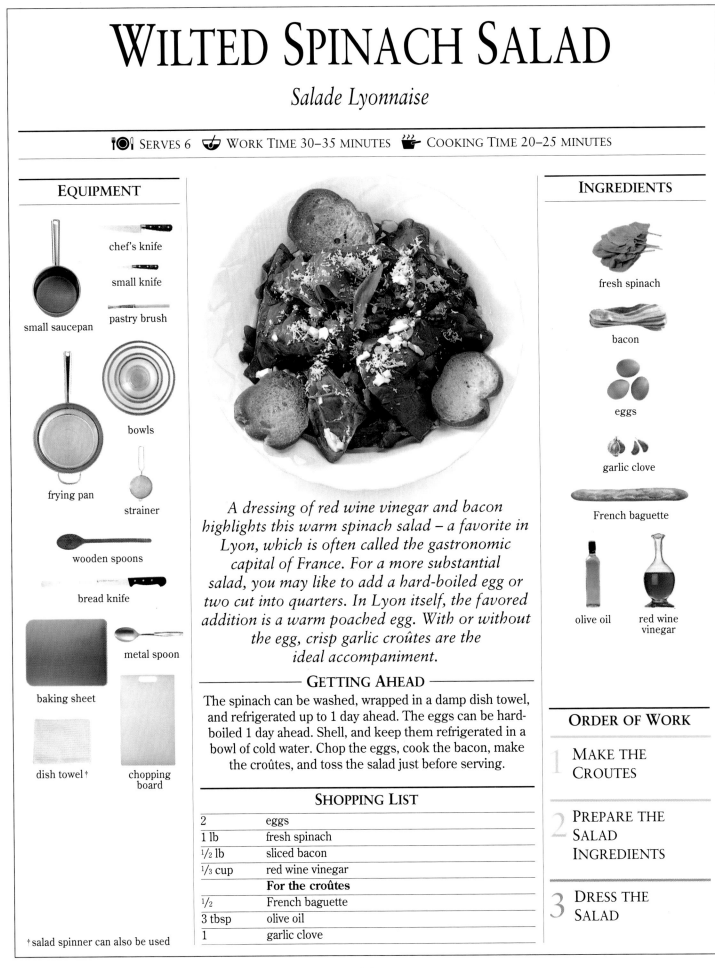

A dressing of red wine vinegar and bacon highlights this warm spinach salad – a favorite in Lyon, which is often called the gastronomic capital of France. For a more substantial salad, you may like to add a hard-boiled egg or two cut into quarters. In Lyon itself, the favored addition is a warm poached egg. With or without the egg, crisp garlic croûtes are the ideal accompaniment.

— GETTING AHEAD —

The spinach can be washed, wrapped in a damp dish towel, and refrigerated up to 1 day ahead. The eggs can be hard-boiled 1 day ahead. Shell, and keep them refrigerated in a bowl of cold water. Chop the eggs, cook the bacon, make the croûtes, and toss the salad just before serving.

SHOPPING LIST

2	eggs
1 lb	fresh spinach
½ lb	sliced bacon
⅓ cup	red wine vinegar
	For the croûtes
½	French baguette
3 tbsp	olive oil
1	garlic clove

INGREDIENTS

fresh spinach

bacon

eggs

garlic clove

French baguette

olive oil   red wine vinegar

ORDER OF WORK

1 MAKE THE CROUTES

2 PREPARE THE SALAD INGREDIENTS

3 DRESS THE SALAD

1 MAKE THE CROUTES

1 Heat the oven to 400°F. Using the bread knife, cut the baguette into ¼-inch slices.

Olive oil flavors bread and makes it crunchy when baked

Cut large garlic clove for rubbing croûtes

2 Brush the olive oil over both sides of each slice of bread, setting the slices on the baking sheet. Bake in the heated oven until toasted and golden brown, turning over the slices once, 7–10 minutes.

3 Strike the garlic clove lightly with the flat of the chef's knife, peel off the skin, and cut the clove in half.

4 Rub one side of each slice of toasted bread with the cut sides of the garlic, and discard the clove. Set the croûtes aside.

2 PREPARE THE SALAD INGREDIENTS

2 Tear the leaves into large pieces. Dry the spinach on the dish towel or in a salad spinner. Put it in a bowl.

Pat spinach leaves with towel to dry thoroughly

1 Hard-boil and shell the eggs (see box, page 38). While the eggs are cooking, discard the tough stems and ribs from the spinach. Wash the leaves in plenty of cold water.

HOW TO HARD-BOIL AND SHELL EGGS

Chopped, sliced, or sieved hard-boiled eggs make an attractive decoration for many dishes.

1 Put the eggs in a saucepan with enough cold water to cover them. Bring to a boil and simmer the eggs, 10 minutes. Remove from the heat and run cold water into the saucepan to stop the eggs cooking.

2 Allow to cool, then drain. Roll or tap each egg on a work surface to crack the shell all over.

3 Remove the shell from each of the eggs. Rinse with cold water, then dry them with paper towels.

3 Separate the egg yolks from the whites by gently pulling the whites apart. Chop the whites. Put the yolks in the strainer set over a bowl; work them through, using the back of the metal spoon. Scrape yolk from bottom of strainer.

Sieved egg yolk retains fluffiness if you take care not to crush it

4 Stack the bacon slices on the chopping board and cut the slices crosswise into strips, using the chef's knife.

ANNE SAYS
"Depending on the type of bacon you use, you may need to discard excess fat, or to add vegetable or olive oil after frying, to make up the quantity needed to dress the spinach."

3 DRESS THE SALAD

Hot bacon and fat will wilt spinach

1 Heat the frying pan, add the bacon and cook, stirring occasionally, until it is crisp and the fat is rendered, 3–5 minutes. Add the bacon, and fat, to the spinach. There should be about ½ cup fat.

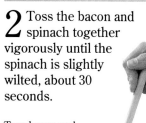

2 Toss the bacon and spinach together vigorously until the spinach is slightly wilted, about 30 seconds.

Toss bacon and spinach with wooden spoons

3 Pour the vinegar into the frying pan. Bring it to a boil, stirring to dissolve the pan juices. Boil it until reduced by one-third, about 1 minute.

! TAKE CARE !
Let the pan cool slightly before adding the vinegar so it does not splutter.

4 Pour the vinegar and pan juices over the spinach and bacon, and toss together well until the spinach is evenly coated in dressing.

Dressing of hot bacon fat and vinegar slightly cooks and wilts spinach leaves

🍴 **TO SERVE**
Pile the salad on 6 individual plates. Sprinkle each serving with the egg white and yolk, and serve at once, with the croûtes.

Garlic croûtes add body to spinach salad

WILTED ESCAROLE SALAD

Peppery escarole is as delicious with a warm bacon dressing as spinach. Parmesan cheese slices replace the sieved egg yolks and chopped egg whites.

1 Omit the garlic croûtes and eggs. Replace the spinach with a 1½-lb head of escarole. Discard the root end and any withered outer leaves. Pull the leaves apart and immerse them in cold water. Discard tough stems, and tear large leaves in half. Dry the leaves on a dish towel or in a salad spinner.
2 Using a vegetable peeler, shave large strips from a 4-oz piece of Parmesan cheese.
3 Fry the bacon as directed in the main recipe, and transfer it to the escarole with a slotted spoon, leaving the fat in the frying pan. Allow the fat to cool slightly, then add ¼ cup pine nuts. Fry the pine nuts, stirring constantly, until they are golden and toasted, 30–60 seconds. Pour them, with the hot fat, over the escarole and toss vigorously. Dissolve the pan juices in vinegar and finish the salad as directed.
4 Arrange the salad on 6 individual plates, with the Parmesan slices. Serve at once, while still warm.

MELON AND MINT SALAD

¡O¡ SERVES 6 **🥄 WORK TIME 15–20 MINUTES***

EQUIPMENT

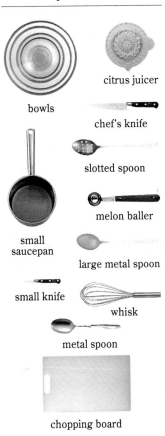

bowls

citrus juicer

chef's knife

slotted spoon

melon baller

small saucepan

large metal spoon

small knife

whisk

metal spoon

chopping board

ANNE SAYS
"Look for a large melon baller to scoop balls of generous size; the best melon ballers have a sharp edge."

A refreshing summer salad of pale green and orange or yellow melon balls with mint and cherry tomatoes, macerated in a sweet and savory dressing. It is ideal as a light first course or to accompany cold cuts on a picnic.

GETTING AHEAD

Melon and mint salad can be made up to 6 hours in advance and kept, covered, in the refrigerator. The dressing can be made up to 1 week ahead and kept in a sealed container in the refrigerator.

*plus 1 hour chilling time

SHOPPING LIST

2	small orange- or yellow-fleshed melons, such as cantaloupe, total weight about 3 lb
1	medium green-fleshed melon, such as honeydew, weighing about 3 lb
³/₄ lb	cherry tomatoes
1	bunch of fresh mint
	For the sweet and savory dressing
¹/₃ cup	port wine
2	lemons
2 tbsp	honey
	salt and pepper

INGREDIENTS

melons

cherry tomatoes

lemons

honey

fresh mint

port wine

ORDER OF WORK

1 **PREPARE THE SALAD INGREDIENTS**

2 **MAKE THE SWEET AND SAVORY DRESSING AND FINISH THE SALAD**

1 PREPARE THE SALAD INGREDIENTS

For neat melon balls push and twist baller deep into melon flesh

Remaining flesh can be used in fruit salad

1 With the chef's knife, halve one of the melons. Scoop out the seeds with a spoon and discard them. Repeat with the remaining melons.

2 Using the melon baller, cut balls from the flesh of each melon half into a large bowl.

3 Scoop out the remaining flesh from the green-fleshed melon halves to make containers for the salad.

ANNE SAYS
"Don't throw away the flesh from the melon shells; use it for a fruit salad."

4 Trim off the melon stalk. Cut each melon shell into 3 wedges, trimming to make the wedges sit flat. Chill the shells until ready to serve.

Cores need not be removed from cherry tomatoes

5 Remove the stems from the cherry tomatoes. Immerse the tomatoes in a saucepan of boiling water until the skins start to split. Transfer them at once to a bowl of cold water. When cold, peel off the skins. Add the tomatoes to the melon balls, reserving six of them.

6 Strip the mint leaves from the stems, reserving some sprigs intact for garnish. Pile the leaves on the chopping board and coarsely chop them. Add the chopped mint to the melon and tomatoes.

2 MAKE THE SWEET AND SAVORY DRESSING AND FINISH THE SALAD

1 Put the port wine in a bowl. Squeeze the juice from the lemons; you should have about 6 tbsp juice.

Lemon juice offsets sweetness of honey and port wine

2 Add the lemon juice, honey, salt, and pepper to the port wine. Whisk the dressing ingredients together. Taste the sweet and savory dressing for seasoning.

3 Pour the dressing over the melon balls, tomatoes, and mint, stir gently, and taste for seasoning.

Mint sprigs set in peeled cherry tomatoes make attractive garnish

4 Cover the bowl, and chill the salad in the refrigerator, so the flavors mellow, about 1 hour.

❮❮❮ TO SERVE
Set the melon shells on a serving plate. Spoon the salad and dressing over them. Decorate with the reserved mint sprigs and peeled cherry tomatoes.

Melon shell makes ideal container

V A R I A T I O N

MELON AND CUCUMBER SALAD

The crispness of cucumber marries well with melon in this salad, which is dotted with red or black grapes. For convenience, try to find seedless grapes, but if the grapes do have seeds, you'll see how to remove them in the box below.

1 Omit the honeydew melon, tomatoes, and mint; halve, seed, and scoop balls from the flesh of 2 small yellow-fleshed melons, such as cantaloupe (total weight about 3 lb), as directed. Discard the melon halves.
2 Wipe and trim 1 cucumber (weighing about ½ lb); peel it, using a vegetable peeler, and reserve 6 strips of peel to decorate individual servings. Cut the cucumber lengthwise in half.
3 Scoop out the seeds from each of the cucumber halves with a teaspoon. Cut each half lengthwise into 3 strips, and then across into chunks.

4 Stem ½ lb seedless red grapes, or stem and seed ½ lb black grapes (see box, below). Combine the melon, cucumber, and grapes in a bowl.
5 Make the dressing as directed. Pour it over the fruit and stir to combine. Taste the salad for seasoning, and chill as directed.
6 Transfer the salad to 6 chilled coupe or stemmed glasses. Loosely knot the reserved strips of cucumber peel, and top each serving with a knot.

HOW TO SEED GRAPES

Many varieties of seedless grapes are now available, but if your grapes have seeds, here are 2 ways to remove them.

To seed with a paper clip
Open a paper clip. Insert the narrow end of the clip at the stem end of the grape. Twist the clip and remove to extract the seeds.

To seed with a knife
Halve the grapes, then flick out the seeds with the tip of a small knife.

V A R I A T I O N

TANGY MELON SALAD

The addition of onion and orange makes a lively melon salad, good served with Mexican dishes or an Indian curry.

1 Omit the tomatoes, mint, and dressing. Use 1 large orange- or yellow-fleshed melon (weighing about 3 lb), and 2 small green-fleshed melons (total weight about 3 lb). Cut the large melon lengthwise in half; scoop out and discard the seeds. Trim off stalk. Cut each half into 3 wedges. Cut the flesh from the shell, leaving the wedges intact. Slice each wedge of flesh across into 1-inch chunks; push each chunk slightly off-center to create a decorative pattern on the shell.
2 Halve, seed, and scoop balls from the green-fleshed melons, as directed in the main recipe. Scrape out any remaining flesh from 1 of the melons; cut the shell into a decorative container for the dressing, if you like, and chill.
3 Cut ½ red onion into fine dice. Cut away the skin and pith from 1 orange, following the curve of the fruit. Working over a bowl to catch the juice, cut out the orange sections: cut down one side of the dividing membrane and scoop out the section. Continue cutting, folding back the membrane like the pages of a book.
4 For the dressing, whisk 1 cup plain yogurt with 1 tbsp honey, and the reserved orange juice. Transfer it to the melon container, if using, or to a bowl.
5 Arrange the salad ingredients and dressing on a serving platter.

BLACK FOREST POTATO SALAD

🍽 SERVES 6–8 🥄 WORK TIME 25–30 MINUTES* 🍲 COOKING TIME 15–20 MINUTES

EQUIPMENT

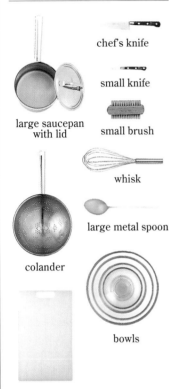

chef's knife

small knife

small brush

large saucepan
with lid

whisk

large metal spoon

colander

bowls

chopping board

INGREDIENTS

red-skinned
new potatoes†

Westphalian
ham

parsley

sour cream

safflower oil‡

small red
onion

caraway
seeds

red wine
vinegar

hot mustard

This potato salad recipe follows a German theme, with slices of boiled new potatoes, slivers of smoked ham from Westphalia, and a piquant vinegar and caraway dressing. The salad is an easy first course to make and an excellent accompaniment to cold cuts.

GETTING AHEAD
The complete salad can be prepared up to 1 day in advance and kept, covered, in the refrigerator. Let the salad come to room temperature before serving.

*plus 1 hour chilling time

† large red-skinned potatoes can also be used

‡ light vegetable oil can also be used

ANNE SAYS
"*Westphalian ham, from Germany, is smoked over juniper twigs and berries. Virginia ham, or any cured ham can be substituted.*"

SHOPPING LIST

3 lb	red-skinned new potatoes
	salt and pepper
5 oz	thinly sliced Westphalian ham
7–10	sprigs of parsley
	For the vinegar and caraway dressing
1	small red onion
3 tbsp	red wine vinegar
3 tbsp	sour cream
2 tbsp	hot mustard
2 tsp	caraway seeds
1 cup	safflower oil

ORDER OF WORK

1 COOK THE
POTATOES AND
MAKE THE
DRESSING

2 ASSEMBLE THE
SALAD

1 COOK THE POTATOES AND MAKE THE DRESSING

1 Using the small brush, scrub the potatoes under cold, running water to remove any dirt, but do not peel them. If using large potatoes, cut each one into 2–4 pieces.

Stiff brush cleans crevices in potato

Potato skins add flavor and color to salad, as well as fiber and nutrients

2 Put the potatoes in the large saucepan with plenty of cold, salted water, cover, and bring to a boil. Simmer just until the potatoes are tender, 15–20 minutes. Meanwhile, make the dressing.

3 Peel the onion, leaving a little of the root attached, and cut it lengthwise in half. Lay each half flat and slice horizontally toward the root, leaving the slices attached at the root end, and then slice vertically. Finally, cut across the onion to make dice. Continue chopping the onion until it is very fine.

Pour oil in slow, steady stream so dressing emulsifies thoroughly

Red onion adds crunch and piquancy to dressing

4 Put the finely chopped onion in a bowl with the vinegar, sour cream, mustard, salt, and pepper. Sprinkle in the caraway seeds.

5 Whisk the ingredients just until mixed, then gradually whisk in the oil so the vinegar and caraway dressing emulsifies and thickens slightly. Taste the dressing for seasoning and set aside.

6 Test the potatoes for tenderness with the tip of the small knife. Drain in the colander, rinse with warm water, and drain again thoroughly.

! TAKE CARE !
If the potatoes are overcooked, they will fall apart when tossed in the dressing.

7 While still warm, cut the potatoes into ¹/₂-inch slices. Transfer the potatoes to a large bowl.

8 Briskly whisk the dressing, then pour it over the warm potatoes. Stir gently so that the potatoes are thoroughly coated. Leave them to cool.

Add dressing to potatoes while they are warm so maximum flavor is absorbed

2 ASSEMBLE THE SALAD

1 While the potatoes cool, trim away fat and any rind from the slices of ham. Cut the ham into ³/₈-inch strips and set aside.

Westphalian ham is normally sold cut into thin slices

HOW TO CHOP HERBS

Parsley, dill, tarragon, rosemary, chives, thyme, and basil are herbs that are usually chopped before being added to other ingredients in a recipe. They can be chopped coarsely or finely, but delicate herbs, such as tarragon and basil, bruise easily, so take care not to chop them too finely.

1 Strip the leaves or sprigs from the stems of the herbs, then pile the leaves or sprigs on a chopping board.

2 Cut the leaves or sprigs into small pieces. Holding the tip of the blade of a chef's knife against the board and rocking the blade back and forth, continue chopping until the herbs are coarse or fine, as you wish.

ANNE SAYS
"Make sure that your knife is very sharp, otherwise you will bruise the herbs rather than cut them."

Parsley gives finishing flavor to salad

2 Coarsely chop the parsley (see box, page 46). Add the ham strips to the cool potato salad. Sprinkle about three-quarters of the parsley over the top. Stir the ham and parsley into the salad. Taste for seasoning, cover, and chill in the refrigerator, at least 1 hour.

TO SERVE
Transfer the potato salad to a large platter and serve at room temperature, sprinkled with the remaining parsley.

Raw red onion adds zing to salad

Smoked ham slivers form tasty partnership with potatoes

VARIATION
YANKEE POTATO SALAD

Enjoyed by Americans far and wide, this salad has many variations. Here is my favorite.

1 Omit the ham and dressing. Cook the new potatoes in their skins, as directed, and cut them into quarters. Put 8 eggs in a medium saucepan, cover them with cold water, bring to a boil and simmer, 10 minutes. Drain the eggs, then let them cool in a bowl of cold water. Tap the eggs to crack the shells, then shell them, and rinse under cold, running water.
2 Cut 4–6 of the eggs into quarters lengthwise and set aside for garnish. Chop the remaining eggs.
3 Stir together ½ cup bottled mayonnaise, ¼ cup sour cream, 3 tbsp red wine vinegar, 1 tbsp Dijon-style mustard, salt, and pepper.
4 Chop the leaves from 1 small bunch of parsley; stir them into the dressing. Taste for seasoning and set aside.

5 Peel the strings from 3 celery stalks with a vegetable peeler. Cut the stalks crosswise to make slices. Drain 2 large dill pickles, cut them into quarters and then crosswise into small pieces. Or, drain ¾ cup gherkin pickles and slice them into thin rounds.

6 Trim 1 small bunch of red radishes, rinse, and cut into thin slices. Finely dice 1 medium onion.
7 Transfer the potatoes to a large bowl. Add the celery, pickles, radishes, onion, and chopped egg. Pour the dressing over the salad, and stir to mix. Taste for seasoning and chill in the refrigerator, at least 1 hour.
8 Serve at room temperature. Garnish individual servings with wedges of egg, and with parsley sprigs, if you like.

SHRIMP AND ZUCCHINI SALAD WITH SAFFRON

🍽 SERVES 6 ⚖ WORK TIME 30–35 MINUTES* 🍲 COOKING TIME 6–10 MINUTES

EQUIPMENT

- frying pan
- bowls
- paper towels
- large metal spoon
- chef's knife
- colander
- pastry brush
- small knife
- 2 shallow, non-metallic dishes
- citrus juicer
- wooden spoon
- plastic wrap
- chopping board

ANNE SAYS
"The marinade contains acidic lemon juice, so do not use metallic dishes to marinate the zucchini and shrimp."

The affinity between shellfish and saffron was recognized 600 years ago in an Italian recipe very similar to this one. Fresh jumbo shrimp, in their shells, are split, then marinated in vinegar, lemon juice, olive oil, capers, and garlic, with a generous pinch of saffron. After broiling, they are served warm, with colorful slices of marinated zucchini.

GETTING AHEAD
The shrimp and zucchini can be marinated up to 6 hours – the longer the time, the stronger the flavor will be. Broil the shrimp and cook the zucchini just before serving.

plus 3–4 hours marinating time

SHOPPING LIST

1	large pinch of saffron threads
2 tbsp	hot water
3	lemons
6	garlic cloves
¼ cup	white wine vinegar
	salt and pepper
1 cup	olive oil, more for broiler rack
⅓ cup	drained capers
1 lb	zucchini
18	raw, unpeeled jumbo shrimp, total weight about 2 lb

INGREDIENTS

- zucchini
- garlic cloves
- raw, unpeeled jumbo shrimp †
- capers
- saffron
- lemons
- white wine vinegar
- olive oil

† striped or tiger prawns can also be used

ANNE SAYS
"Saffron is the dried stamen of the autumn crocus, and the best saffron comes in threads, as illustrated, not powder."

ORDER OF WORK

1 **MAKE THE MARINADE**

2 **MARINATE THE ZUCCHINI AND SHRIMP**

3 **COOK THE ZUCCHINI AND SHRIMP; ASSEMBLE THE SALAD**

1 MAKE THE MARINADE

1 Put the saffron threads in a medium bowl and pour the hot water over them. Let stand, 5 minutes.

2 Squeeze the juice from 2 of the lemons. There should be about 6 tbsp juice. Set the flat side of the chef's knife on top of each garlic clove and strike it with your fist. Discard the skin and coarsely chop the garlic.

3 Add the garlic, vinegar, salt, pepper, lemon juice, olive oil, and capers to the saffron and its liquid. Stir together the marinade ingredients, lightly crushing the capers against the side of the bowl to extract their flavor.

After soaking in hot water, saffron yields brilliant golden color

2 MARINATE THE ZUCCHINI AND SHRIMP

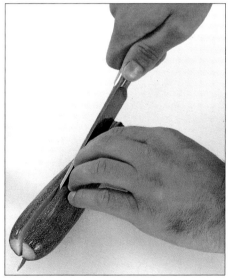

1 Trim the zucchini, discarding the ends. Cut each one lengthwise in half with the chef's knife.

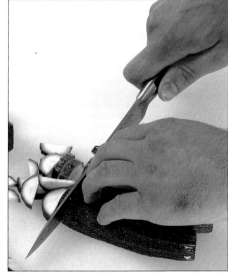

2 Set the halves, two by two, flat-side down on the chopping board, and cut crosswise into 1/4-inch slices.

3 Transfer the zucchini to a shallow dish. Spoon two-thirds of the marinade over the zucchini. Toss to coat, cover, and transfer to the refrigerator to marinate, 3–4 hours. Reserve the remaining marinade for the shrimp.

4 Hold each shrimp, underside up, on the chopping board. Leaving the tail end intact, cut each shrimp in half to open in a butterfly shape.

Shells will trap succulent juices when shrimp are broiled

Dry shrimp well so marinade is not diluted

5 Pull out and discard the dark intestinal vein running along the back of each shrimp.

6 Rinse the butterflied shrimp under cold, running water in the colander. Carefully transfer the shrimp to paper towels on the work surface, and pat them dry.

7 Put the shrimp in the second non-metallic dish, spoon the remaining marinade over the top, and toss to coat. Cover, and transfer to the refrigerator to marinate, 3–4 hours.

3 COOK THE ZUCCHINI AND SHRIMP; ASSEMBLE THE SALAD

2 Meanwhile, heat the broiler. With the pastry brush, oil the broiler rack. Take each shrimp from the marinade and set it, cut-side up, on the broiler rack.

Spread shrimp flat so they cook evenly

1 Heat the frying pan, then add the zucchini to the frying pan with the marinade. Simmer, stirring, just until tender, 3–5 minutes.

3 Brush each shrimp with a little marinade. Spoon the capers remaining in the dish over the shrimp, retaining some marinade to brush over the shrimp while broiling.

To keep shrimp moist, brush with marinade during cooking

4 Broil the shrimp about 2 inches from the heat until pink and sizzling, 3–4 minutes. Slice the remaining lemon into thin wedges.

! TAKE CARE !
Do not overcook the shrimp or they will be tough to eat.

¶◎¶ TO SERVE
Pile the warm zucchini in the center of each plate, discarding the marinade. Surround with shrimp; garnish with the lemon wedges.

Golden color
of zucchini
comes from
saffron marinade

Butterflied shrimp
make attractive
presentation

V A R I A T I O N

MARINATED SHRIMP AND MUSHROOM SALAD

Button mushrooms, which replace the sliced zucchini, are served in a simple antipasto-style salad with the shrimp.

1 Prepare the marinade as directed in the main recipe, omitting the saffron. Butterfly and devein the unpeeled shrimp as directed. Marinate the butterflied shrimp as directed, using only one-third of the marinade.
2 Omit the zucchini. Wipe the caps of $3/4$ lb button mushrooms with damp paper towels, and trim the stems even with the caps. If necessary, cut large mushrooms into quarters. Bring a small pan of salted water to a boil, add the mushrooms, and simmer just until tender, 5–7 minutes. Drain, rinse under cold water, and drain again. Add the mushrooms to the remaining marinade, stir, cover, and transfer to the refrigerator to marinate, 3–4 hours.
3 Using a slotted spoon, divide the mushrooms among 6 individual plates, discarding the marinade.
4 Heat the broiler and broil the shrimp as directed. Transfer the broiled butterflied shrimp to the plates and serve immediately. If you like, decorate each serving with a lemon wedge and flat-leaf parsley sprig.

CREAMY COLESLAW

EQUIPMENT

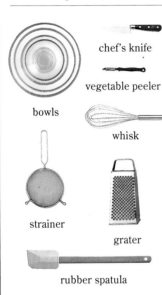

chef's knife

vegetable peeler

bowls

whisk

strainer

grater

rubber spatula

chopping board

mandoline †

† food processor with slicing blade can also be used

Coleslaw literally means "cabbage salad," no matter how you slice it, but there are many variations on the theme. Here, green cabbage is finely shredded and tossed with a sour cream dressing pepped up with mustard powder and caraway seeds. Grated carrot is added for color, together with carrot curls for an appetizing garnish. This recipe makes a generous quantity for a party, or it can be halved easily.

— GETTING AHEAD —

Coleslaw can be made 2 days in advance and kept, covered, in the refrigerator.

plus minimum 4 hours chilling time

INGREDIENTS

carrots

green cabbage

onion

cider vinegar

sugar

bottled mayonnaise

sour cream

mustard powder

caraway seeds†

†celery seeds can also be used

SHOPPING LIST

1 lb	medium carrots
1	medium head of green cabbage, weighing about 3 lb
1	medium onion
	For the sour cream dressing
2 tbsp	sugar
	salt and pepper
1 cup	sour cream
1 cup	cider vinegar
2 tsp	mustard powder
2 tsp	caraway seeds
1 cup	bottled mayonnaise

ORDER OF WORK

1. **PREPARE THE SALAD INGREDIENTS**

2. **MAKE THE SOUR CREAM DRESSING AND FINISH THE SALAD**

1 PREPARE THE SALAD INGREDIENTS

1 Trim and peel the carrots. Using the coarse side of the grater, grate all but 1 of the carrots.

2 Using the vegetable peeler, peel curls from the length of the remaining carrot, discarding the central core. Put the carrot curls in a bowl of cold water, and refrigerate so that they remain crisp.

Mandoline shreds cabbage finely and evenly

3 Trim the cabbage and discard any wilted leaves. Cut it in half, then into quarters, and cut out the core. Shred each quarter into a large bowl using the mandoline, discarding any thick ribs. Alternatively, shred the cabbage in a food processor, using the slicing blade.

4 Peel the onion, leaving a little of the root attached, and cut it lengthwise in half. Lay each onion half flat and slice horizontally toward the root, leaving the slices attached at the root end, and then slice vertically, again leaving the root end uncut. Finally, cut across to make fine dice.

2 MAKE THE SOUR CREAM DRESSING AND FINISH THE SALAD

1 Put the sugar, salt, pepper, sour cream, and cider vinegar in a medium bowl. Add the mustard powder and caraway seeds.

Sour cream makes thick dressing

Mustard gives hot bite to coleslaw

2 Whisk the sour cream dressing ingredients together to combine them thoroughly.

Choose bowl
large enough for
ingredients to be
tossed easily with
dressing

3 Add the mayonnaise to the sour cream dressing and whisk to combine. Taste for seasoning.

4 Add the diced onion and grated carrot to the shredded cabbage in the bowl.

5 Pour the sour cream dressing over the salad, and stir until coated. Cover, and chill in the refrigerator, so that the flavors mellow, at least 4 hours. Taste the salad for seasoning.

Finely shredded cabbage
is coated with thick and
creamy dressing

Grated carrot
complements cabbage

6 Remove the carrot curls from the refrigerator and drain them in the strainer set over a bowl.

 TO SERVE
Uncover the coleslaw and stir once more to coat the salad well. Divide the salad among individual bowls. Garnish each serving with carrot curls.

Carrot curls add
color to salad

APPLE AND PINEAPPLE COLESLAW

In this version of coleslaw, shredded cabbage is mixed with grated apple and crushed pineapple for a tart, fruity flavor. A fresh salad like this is particularly good with rich meats, such as pork and barbecued ribs.

1 Omit the carrot, onion, and dressing. Shred the cabbage as directed.

2 Drain a 1¼-lb can crushed pineapple in natural juice. Grate 4 unpeeled, tart green apples, such as Granny Smith, and put them in a large bowl.

3 Add the pineapple to the apples, and stir so that the pineapple juice thoroughly coats the apples, preventing them from discoloring.

4 In a small bowl, stir together ⅔ cup cider vinegar, 1 cup buttermilk, 1 cup bottled mayonnaise, 2 tsp mustard powder, salt, and pepper. Taste the dressing for seasoning.

5 Add the shredded cabbage to the apple and pineapple mixture in the large bowl and combine.

6 Pour the dressing over the salad and stir to mix. Taste the coleslaw for seasoning. Cover, and chill in the refrigerator, as directed.

7 If you like, garnish each serving with an apple chevron (see page 125).

Buttermilk dressing coats crushed pineapple, apples, and cabbage

GREEN AND RED CABBAGE COLESLAW

Red cabbage replaces the carrot in this version of Creamy Coleslaw, creating a colorful presentation. This is a winter salad, ideal with cold roast beef, or the leftovers of the holiday turkey.

1 Omit the carrots. Shred the green cabbage as directed.

2 Shred ½ head of red cabbage (weighing about 1½ lb) as directed. Heat a large saucepan of salted water to boiling. Add the red cabbage, bring back to a boil, and simmer, 1 minute.

3 Drain the red cabbage in a colander. While it is still hot, sprinkle with ¼ cup red wine vinegar. Toss to mix, and let drain in the colander. Chop the onion as directed.

4 Omit the cider vinegar. Squeeze the juice from 3 lemons; there should be about ½ cup juice. Make the dressing as directed, using the lemon juice in place of vinegar.

5 Combine the shredded green and red cabbage in a large bowl.

6 Pour the dressing over the salad. Stir the green and red cabbage coleslaw and taste for seasoning. Cover, and chill in the refrigerator, as directed.

7 Transfer the coleslaw to a large serving platter.

Classic Caesar Salad

🍽 Serves 6–8 🥄 Work Time 20–25 minutes 🍲 Cooking Time 2–3 minutes

EQUIPMENT

paper towels

grater

large frying pan

bread knife

bowls

colander

chef's knife

dish towel†

strainer

whisk

chopping board

† salad spinner can also be used

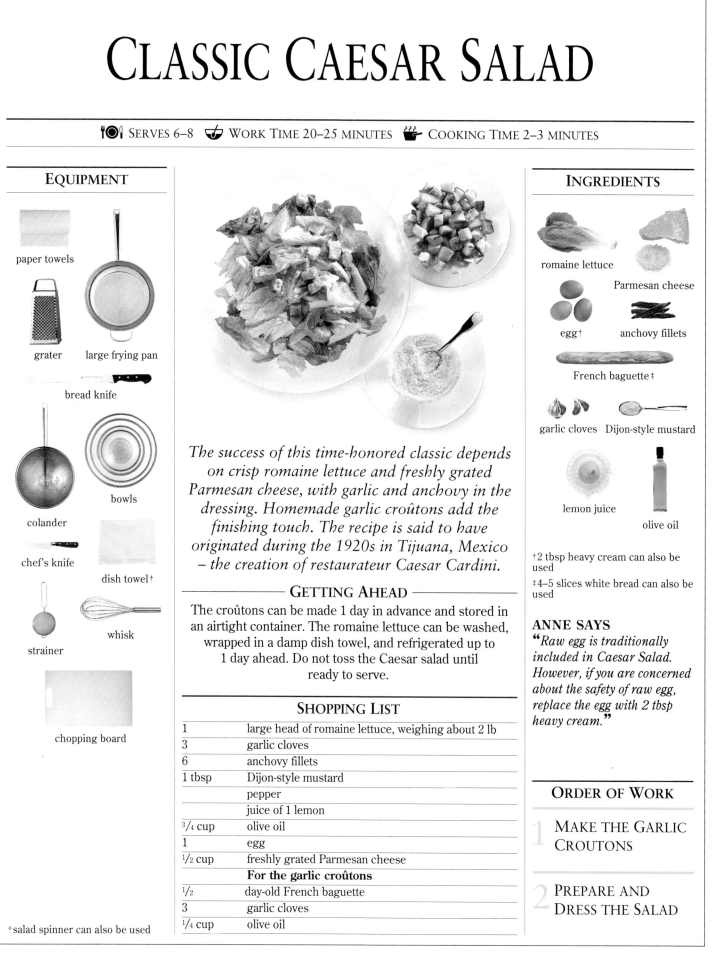

The success of this time-honored classic depends on crisp romaine lettuce and freshly grated Parmesan cheese, with garlic and anchovy in the dressing. Homemade garlic croûtons add the finishing touch. The recipe is said to have originated during the 1920s in Tijuana, Mexico – the creation of restaurateur Caesar Cardini.

GETTING AHEAD

The croûtons can be made 1 day in advance and stored in an airtight container. The romaine lettuce can be washed, wrapped in a damp dish towel, and refrigerated up to 1 day ahead. Do not toss the Caesar salad until ready to serve.

SHOPPING LIST

1	large head of romaine lettuce, weighing about 2 lb
3	garlic cloves
6	anchovy fillets
1 tbsp	Dijon-style mustard
	pepper
	juice of 1 lemon
3/4 cup	olive oil
1	egg
1/2 cup	freshly grated Parmesan cheese
	For the garlic croûtons
1/2	day-old French baguette
3	garlic cloves
1/4 cup	olive oil

INGREDIENTS

romaine lettuce

Parmesan cheese

egg†

anchovy fillets

French baguette ‡

garlic cloves Dijon-style mustard

lemon juice

olive oil

† 2 tbsp heavy cream can also be used

‡ 4–5 slices white bread can also be used

ANNE SAYS
"*Raw egg is traditionally included in Caesar Salad. However, if you are concerned about the safety of raw egg, replace the egg with 2 tbsp heavy cream.*"

ORDER OF WORK

1 MAKE THE GARLIC CROUTONS

2 PREPARE AND DRESS THE SALAD

1 MAKE THE GARLIC CROUTONS

Leave crust on French bread for crisp croûtons to complement other salad ingredients

French bread slices will be transformed into golden croûtons

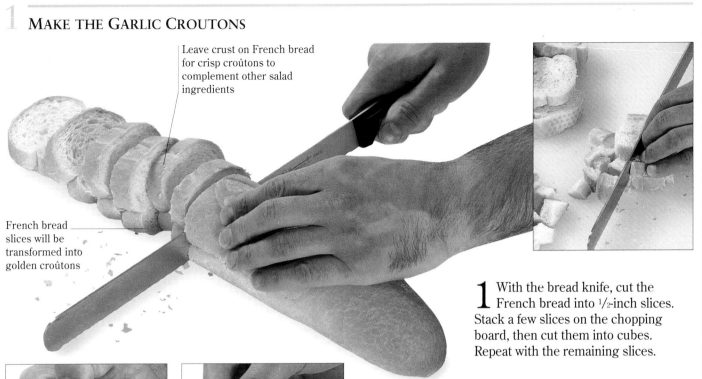

1 With the bread knife, cut the French bread into ½-inch slices. Stack a few slices on the chopping board, then cut them into cubes. Repeat with the remaining slices.

2 Set the flat side of the chef's knife on top of each garlic clove; strike it with your fist to loosen skin.

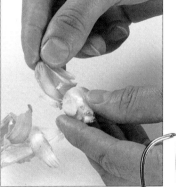

3 Pull off and discard the skin from each of the garlic cloves.

Fried croûtons are subtly flavored by garlic cloves

4 Heat the oil in the large frying pan. Add the garlic cloves and bread cubes, and fry, stirring constantly, until the croûtons are golden, about 2–3 minutes.

5 Tip the croûtons out of the frying pan onto paper towels to drain. Discard the garlic cloves.

ANNE SAYS
"Croûtons will retain their crispness if drained thoroughly."

2 PREPARE AND DRESS THE SALAD

2 Discard any tough stems, and then tear the lettuce leaves into small pieces. Dry the lettuce on the dish towel. Peel and finely chop the garlic cloves.

To avoid bruising them, tear lettuce leaves with your fingers rather than using a knife

1 Twist, pull off, and discard the root end from the lettuce. Wash the leaves in plenty of cold water, then rinse each leaf under cold, running water.

3 Drain the anchovy fillets, put them in a large salad bowl, and crush them with the tines of a table fork.

4 Add the garlic, mustard, and pepper. Pour in the lemon juice; stir the dressing ingredients with the whisk.

Salad is easy to toss in bowl if you use your hands

Piquant dressing peps up salad leaves

5 Gradually whisk in the oil so the anchovy dressing emulsifies and thickens slightly. Taste the dressing for seasoning.

6 Add the lettuce to the dressing and toss until the leaves are well coated.

7 Crack the egg into a small bowl, then add it to the salad leaves and dressing, and toss together until thoroughly mixed.

Egg helps bind salad together while adding richness

Romaine lettuce is an essential ingredient in this salad

8 Add half of the garlic croûtons, and two-thirds of the Parmesan cheese, and toss the salad again. Taste a piece of lettuce for seasoning, adding salt only if necessary; the cheese and anchovies are already salty.

🍽 **TO SERVE**
Serve the salad directly from the salad bowl and pass the remaining Parmesan cheese and croûtons separately.

Parmesan cheese enhances flavor of salad

V A R I A T I O N

CAESAR SALAD WITH TOMATOES AND ASPARAGUS

The intense flavor of sun-dried tomatoes replaces that of anchovies in this variation.

1 Make the garlic croûtons as directed in the main recipe.
2 Using a vegetable peeler, strip away the tough outer skins from 3/4 lb asparagus stems; trim off the woody ends. Tie the stems into 2–3 bundles with kitchen string. Bring a large saucepan of salted water to a boil, add the asparagus, and simmer just until tender when pierced with a knife, 5–7 minutes. Drain, rinse with cold water, and drain again.
3 Cut off about 2 inches of the tips and reserve. Cut the asparagus stems into 3/4-inch pieces.
4 Cut out the cores from 2 lb plum tomatoes, and cut each tomato crosswise into 1/4-inch slices.
5 Omit the anchovy fillets. Drain and finely chop 1/4 cup oil-soaked sun-dried tomatoes. Prepare the salad as directed, adding the sun-dried tomatoes in place of the anchovies.
6 Toss the asparagus stems with the lettuce, two-thirds of the Parmesan, and half of the croûtons. Taste for seasoning and arrange on individual plates. Garnish with the tomato slices, reserved asparagus tips, croûtons, and cheese.

AVOCADO AND GRAPEFRUIT SALAD WITH PROSCIUTTO

🍴 SERVES 4   ⌣ WORK TIME 25–30 MINUTES

EQUIPMENT

grater

bowls

vegetable peeler

salad spinner†

pastry brush

chef's knife

small saucepan

strainer

whisk

chopping board

† dish towel can also be used

This wheel of overlapping grapefruit sections and avocado slices is speckled with honey and poppy-seed vinaigrette dressing and decorated with grapefruit julienne. Prosciutto and bitter greens, such as arugula, add a pleasant contrast of flavor.

GETTING AHEAD

The grapefruit sections and julienne can be prepared 1 day ahead, and kept, covered, in the refrigerator. You can also make the dressing 1 day ahead. Assemble the salad not more than 30 minutes before serving and be sure the avocado is thoroughly sprinkled with grapefruit juice so it does not discolor.

SHOPPING LIST

4	grapefruit
4 oz	thinly sliced prosciutto
6 oz	arugula
2	avocados
	For the poppy-seed vinaigrette dressing
1/2	small onion
3 tbsp	red wine vinegar
1 tbsp	honey
1/2 tsp	mustard powder
1/4 tsp	ground ginger
	salt and pepper
2/3 cup	vegetable oil
1 tbsp	poppy seeds

INGREDIENTS

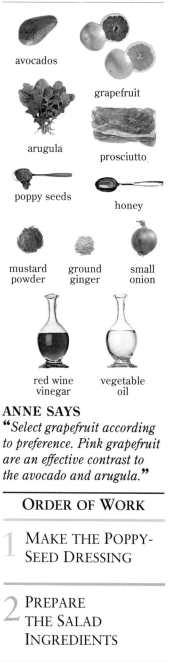

avocados

grapefruit

arugula

prosciutto

poppy seeds

honey

mustard powder

ground ginger

small onion

red wine vinegar

vegetable oil

ANNE SAYS
"Select grapefruit according to preference. Pink grapefruit are an effective contrast to the avocado and arugula."

ORDER OF WORK

1 MAKE THE POPPY-SEED DRESSING

2 PREPARE THE SALAD INGREDIENTS

3 ASSEMBLE THE SALAD

1 MAKE THE POPPY-SEED DRESSING

Grated onion adds piquancy to dressing

1 Using the coarse or fine side of the grater, grate the onion half into a bowl.

2 Add the vinegar, honey, mustard powder, ground ginger, salt, and pepper to the grated onion and whisk together. Gradually whisk in the oil so the vinaigrette dressing emulsifies and thickens slightly.

3 Add the poppy seeds, and whisk them into the vinaigrette dressing. Taste the dressing for seasoning, and adjust if necessary.

2 PREPARE THE SALAD INGREDIENTS

1 Using the vegetable peeler, pare half of the zest from 1 of the grapefruit, leaving behind the white pith. Cut the pared zest into very fine julienne strips with the chef's knife.

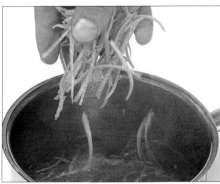

2 Half-fill the small saucepan with water and bring to a boil. Add the grapefruit julienne, simmer 2 minutes, drain, and set aside.

Fold back dividing membrane as you cut out each section

3 Slice off the top and base of the grapefruit. Cut away the zest, pith, and skin, following the curve of the fruit. Repeat with each of the remaining grapefruit.

4 Holding each grapefruit over a bowl, cut out the sections: slide the knife down each side of a section to cut it free of the membranes. Release the section into the bowl.

5 Repeat with the remaining sections, turning the membranes back like the pages of a book; discard seeds as you go. Cover the sections and juice, and chill in the refrigerator.

6 Cut the prosciutto slices across into 1-inch strips, cutting off and discarding any fat or rind.

Lift arugula leaves out of water so any grit is left behind

7 Separate the arugula leaves and immerse them in a sink full of cold water, 15–30 minutes. Rinse the leaves in plenty of cold water, and drain them well. Dry the arugula in the salad spinner or on a dish towel.

Cold water crisps arugula leaves but be sure to dry them thoroughly because wet leaves dilute dressing

8 Cut lengthwise around each avocado, through to the pit. Twist with both hands to loosen the halves and pull them apart.

9 With a chopping movement, embed the blade of the chef's knife in the avocado pit and lift it free of the avocado. Alternatively, scoop out the avocado pit with a spoon.

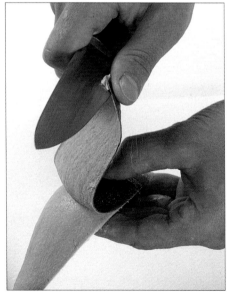

10 Cut the avocado into quarters and strip off the skin, using the chef's knife. Cut each quarter into lengthwise slices. Prepare the second avocado in the same way.

Brushing with acidic grapefruit juice keeps avocado slices from discoloring

11 Brush the reserved grapefruit juice over the avocado slices so that they do not discolor.

3 ASSEMBLE THE SALAD

Arugula leaves are tossed in dressing before being arranged on plate

Arugula leaves create attractive border

1 Briskly whisk the poppy-seed dressing. Toss the arugula with one-third of the dressing and taste for seasoning. Spread a bed of arugula on 4 plates. Arrange the avocado slices and grapefruit sections like the spokes of a wheel on top. Curl the prosciutto strips into cones and place in the center.

2 Spoon the remaining poppy-seed vinaigrette dressing over each individual serving.

🍽 **TO SERVE**
Sprinkle the grapefruit julienne over the top of each serving.

Grapefruit julienne makes dainty decoration

Sweet and juicy grapefruit contrasts with avocado and arugula

V A R I A T I O N

AVOCADO AND GRAPEFRUIT SALAD WITH SMOKED SALMON

Delicate smoked salmon replaces the prosciutto in this variation – perfect for a Sunday brunch.

1 Omit the prosciutto. Strip the leaves from 5 sprigs of fresh dill and pile them on a chopping board. With a chef's knife, finely chop the leaves. Make the dressing as directed in the main recipe, and whisk in the dill. Section 4 white grapefruit, omitting the zest.

2 Cut 6 oz sliced smoked salmon into 2-inch strips. Prepare 3 oz arugula as directed. Cut the root end from 1 small head of radicchio (weighing about 3 oz), and discard any withered leaves. Separate and wash the leaves in plenty of cold water. Dry the radicchio in a salad spinner or on a dish towel.

3 Toss the arugula and radicchio leaves in the salad dressing and alternate them on 4 individual plates. Arrange the grapefruit sections and avocado slices in a loose spoke pattern on top. Curl salmon strips to form a rose in the center of each serving, and garnish with dill sprigs, if you like.

INDONESIAN SALAD

Gado Gado

🍽 SERVES 8   🥣 WORK TIME 35–45 MINUTES*   🍲 COOKING TIME 20–25 MINUTES

EQUIPMENT

bowls

food processor †

wooden spoon

colander

metal spatula

chef's knife

small knife

cheesecloth

vegetable peeler

strainer   large frying pan

saucepans, 1 with lid

rubber spatula

chopping board

† blender can also be used

INGREDIENTS

cauliflower   eggs

bean sprouts   cucumbers

carrots

soy sauce   garlic cloves

onion

shelled roasted   tofu
peanuts

hot red
pepper   vegetable
flakes   lime juice   oil

brown   shredded
sugar   coconut

Traditionally, this salad combines a variety of
fresh vegetables. The accompanying peanut sauce
can be made spicy or sweet to your taste.

GETTING AHEAD

The vegetables can be blanched and the peanut sauce can
be made 1 day ahead and kept, covered, in the refrigerator.
Let the vegetables come to room temperature before serving.

plus 30 minutes standing time for coconut

SHOPPING LIST

1	small head of cauliflower, weighing about 1½ lb
	salt and pepper
1 lb	medium carrots
1 lb	cucumbers
¾ lb	bean sprouts
10 oz	tofu
3	eggs
1 tbsp	vegetable oil
	For the peanut sauce
1½ cups	water
1½ cups	unsweetened shredded coconut
½ cup	vegetable oil
½ lb	shelled roasted peanuts
3	garlic cloves
1	medium onion
½ tsp	hot red pepper flakes
1 tbsp	soy sauce
	juice of 1 lime
2 tsp	brown sugar

ORDER OF WORK

1 PREPARE THE
VEGETABLES
AND TOFU

2 MAKE THE
OMELET GARNISH

3 MAKE THE
PEANUT SAUCE
AND ASSEMBLE
THE SALAD

1 PREPARE THE VEGETABLES AND TOFU

1 Trim the florets from the head of cauliflower. Cut large florets in half or quarters.

Tough leaves and stems are discarded

Cauliflower florets should be similar in size to one another

2 Bring a large saucepan of salted water to a boil. Add the florets and boil just until tender, 5–7 minutes. Drain, rinse with cold water, and drain again thoroughly.

3 Peel the carrots and trim off the ends. Cut each carrot crosswise into 2-inch lengths. Square off the sides of each piece of carrot.

4 Using the chef's knife, cut each piece lengthwise into 1/8-inch slices. Stack the slices on the chopping board and cut each stack lengthwise into 1/8-inch sticks.

5 Put the carrots in a medium saucepan of cold, salted water. Bring to a boil and simmer the carrots just until tender, 3–5 minutes. Drain, rinse with cold water, and drain again.

6 Peel the cucumbers and trim off the ends. Cut them lengthwise in half and scoop out the seeds from each half with a teaspoon.

Peel cucumbers in case they have been waxed

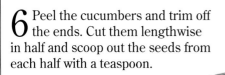

Vegetable peeler ensures minimum wastage of cucumber

7 Cut the halves lengthwise into 1/4-inch strips, then gather the strips into a bundle and cut across into 2-inch sticks.

Tofu is made from the popular Asian soybean

8 Pick over the bean sprouts and put in a bowl. Cover with boiling water and let stand, 1 minute. Drain.

9 Drain the tofu in the strainer and discard the liquid; cut the tofu into ½-inch cubes, using the chef's knife.

2 MAKE THE OMELET GARNISH

Swirl pan when adding eggs, so they cover base evenly

Egg mixture starts cooking immediately in hot oil

1 Beat the eggs in a small bowl with salt and pepper to taste. Heat the oil in the frying pan. Pour in the beaten eggs, tilting the pan so that they spread into an even layer. Cook the omelet over medium heat until the edge appears slightly crispy and pulls away from the side, about 2 minutes.

2 With the metal spatula, lift and turn the omelet over. Cook until firm, about 30 seconds.

Sliced, rolled omelet makes attractive garnish

3 Slide the omelet out of the pan onto the chopping board. Let it cool slightly. Roll up the omelet loosely.

4 Cut the omelet crosswise into curled strips. Set aside while preparing the vegetables.

HOW TO CHOP AN ONION

The size of dice when chopping an onion depends on the thickness of the initial slices. For a standard size, make slices that are about 1/4-inch thick. For finely chopped onions, slice as thinly as possible.

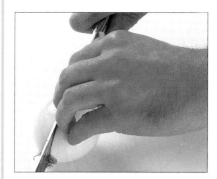

1 Peel the onion and trim the top, leaving the root intact. Cut the onion lengthwise in half, through root and stem.

2 Put one half, cut-side down, on the chopping board, and hold it steady with one hand. Using a chef's knife, slice horizontally toward the root, leaving the slices attached at the root end.

3 Slice the onion half vertically, again leaving the root end uncut. Finally, cut across the onion to make dice.

3 MAKE THE PEANUT SAUCE AND ASSEMBLE THE SALAD

1 Bring the water to a boil in a small saucepan. Add the coconut and stir to mix, then cover and remove from heat. Let stand, about 30 minutes.

2 Meanwhile, heat half of the oil in the frying pan. Add the peanuts and cook, stirring constantly, until browned, 3–5 minutes.

Peanuts are browned to enhance flavor

3 Transfer the browned peanuts to the food processor. Work the peanuts, using the pulse button. The finished texture of the peanuts should be slightly chunky. If using a blender, work the nuts in 2 batches.

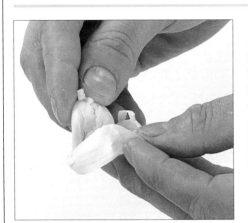

4 Set the flat side of the chef's knife on top of each garlic clove and strike it with your fist. Discard the skin, and finely chop the garlic. Peel and chop the onion (see box, page 67).

5 Heat the remaining oil in the frying pan. Add the onion and cook, stirring, until lightly browned, 2–3 minutes. Add the garlic and hot red pepper flakes, and continue cooking until the onion is golden, about 2 minutes longer. Add the soy sauce, pour in the lime juice, and stir to mix.

Freshly squeezed lime juice is piquant flavor in sauce

Essential flavor is extracted from coconut by infusing in boiling water

6 Remove the pan from the heat. Stir in the brown sugar and ground peanuts. Let cool slightly.

7 Put a large piece of cheesecloth in the strainer, set over a bowl. Pour in the coconut and its liquid from the saucepan.

Cheesecloth is good for straining

8 Gather up the ends of the cheesecloth in your hand and squeeze the coconut well to extract as much liquid or "milk" as possible. Discard the coconut.

9 Gradually add the coconut milk to the peanut sauce, and stir until the sauce is smooth and creamy. Season to taste.

Mixture is quite stiff until coconut milk is added

ANNE SAYS
"*Peanut sauce may separate on standing. If so, heat it gently, and stir in 1–2 tbsp water to re-emulsify it.*"

TO SERVE
Arrange the bean sprouts on a serving plate, top with carrots, cucumbers, and tofu, and crown with the cauliflower florets. Garnish with the omelet curls. Serve peanut sauce separately.

Spicy peanut sauce is delicious accompaniment

Cauliflower florets crown salad

VARIATION

BIRD'S NEST SALAD WITH PEANUT SAUCE

Crunchy red cabbage and green beans add brilliant color to this version of Indonesian Salad.

1 Omit the cauliflower, carrots, cucumbers, omelet, and tofu. Peel 1 lb potatoes, and cut them into 2–4 pieces if large. Put the potatoes in a medium saucepan of salted water, cover, and bring to a boil. Simmer just until they are tender, 15–20 minutes. Drain, rinse with cold water, and drain again thoroughly. Cut into 1/2-inch chunks.

2 Make the peanut sauce as directed in the main recipe.

3 Snap off the ends of 3/4 lb green beans, pulling away any strings from each side. Cut the beans diagonally into 1-inch slices. Cook in boiling, salted water just until tender, 5–8 minutes. Drain, rinse with cold water, and drain again thoroughly.

4 Trim 1/2 head of red cabbage. Cut it in half and cut out the core from each piece. Set the cabbage cut-side down and finely shred it. Discard any thick ribs.

5 Cook the cabbage in boiling, salted water, 1 minute. Drain and toss, while still hot, with 1/4 cup red wine vinegar.

6 Prepare the bean sprouts as directed, then divide them among 8 individual plates. Top with red cabbage. Arrange the green beans in the center, then pile the potatoes in the center of the nest. Add the peanut sauce.

FANTASIA SALAD WITH CHEESE WAFERS

EQUIPMENT

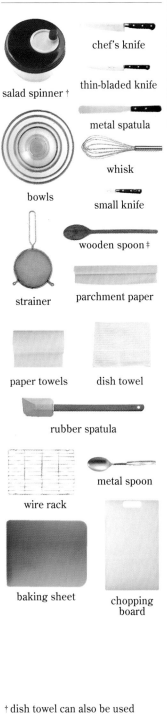

salad spinner †

chef's knife

thin-bladed knife

metal spatula

whisk

bowls

small knife

wooden spoon ‡

strainer

parchment paper

paper towels

dish towel

rubber spatula

wire rack

metal spoon

baking sheet

chopping board

† dish towel can also be used

‡ electric mixer can also be used

The three different salad greens suggested here can be varied. I like to use mesclun, *a mixture of peppery and sweet greens, with leaves in a wide variety of shapes and colors. Typically,* mesclun *includes curly endive, red-leaf lettuce, lamb's lettuce, radicchio, and perhaps some dandelion and arugula leaves, and the herb, chervil.*

*plus 1–2 hours freezing time for cheese wafer dough

SHOPPING LIST

1	head of red-leaf lettuce, weighing about ½ lb
1	head of Boston lettuce, weighing about ½ lb
½ lb	small spinach leaves
1	small bunch of flat-leaf or curly parsley
6	fresh figs
½ cup	hazelnuts
	For the cheese wafers
4 oz	Stilton, Danish blue, or Roquefort cheese, chilled
4 oz	Saga blue or Bresse Bleu cheese, chilled
½ cup	butter, at room temperature
¾ cup	flour
	For the raspberry dressing
5 oz	fresh raspberries
⅓ cup	raspberry vinegar
⅓ cup	bottled mayonnaise
2 tbsp	heavy cream
	salt and pepper
1 tbsp	hazelnut oil

INGREDIENTS

red-leaf lettuce

Boston lettuce

blue cheeses

bottled mayonnaise

spinach

raspberry vinegar

butter

fresh figs

heavy cream

hazelnut oil

flour

hazelnuts

flat-leaf parsley

raspberries

ORDER OF WORK

1   MAKE THE CHEESE WAFER DOUGH

2   MAKE THE RASPBERRY DRESSING; WASH THE SALAD LEAVES

3   TOAST THE NUTS; BAKE THE WAFERS; FINISH THE SALAD

1 MAKE THE CHEESE WAFER DOUGH

1 With the chef's knife, cut each of the chilled cheeses into chunks, discarding the rind. Allow the cheeses to come to room temperature.

ANNE SAYS
"Choose your favorite blue cheeses for the cheese wafers, but make sure one is crumbly and the other creamy."

Cheese is easy to chop if chilled in refrigerator

Choose one crumbly blue cheese

2 Beat the butter in a medium bowl until softened. Add the chunks of blue cheese to the butter.

3 Beat the chunks of cheese into the butter with the wooden spoon, until they are evenly blended in and the mixture is creamy and smooth.

5 Set a 12- x 12-inch piece of parchment paper on a work surface. Transfer the dough to the paper, and spread the dough evenly along the length of the paper.

Cheese wafer dough is rich and creamy

4 Add the flour to the butter and cheese mixture, and stir the dough with the wooden spoon just until it comes together.

6 Roll the paper tightly around the dough, shaping it into a cylinder 1½-inches in diameter. Twist the ends of the paper to seal them. Put the dough in the freezer until firm, 1–2 hours. Meanwhile, make the raspberry dressing and prepare the salad.

Twist parchment paper ends to seal before chilling

Cheese mixture is sticky, so shape with paper

2 MAKE THE RASPBERRY DRESSING; WASH THE SALAD LEAVES

1 Pick over the raspberries; wash them only if they are dirty. Sieve half of the raspberries through the strainer over a bowl, pressing with the back of a spoon to extract the pulp. Scrape the pulp clinging to the bottom of the strainer into the bowl.

2 Add the vinegar, mayonnaise, cream, salt, pepper, and oil to the raspberry pulp; whisk until combined.

Do not waste raspberry pulp on bottom of strainer

Sieved raspberries form basis of unusual dressing

3 Twist off the core from the red-leaf lettuce, and separate the leaves. Wash the leaves in cold water. Rinse each leaf under running water, discard the tough stems, and tear the leaves into large pieces. Dry in the salad spinner and put in a large bowl.

Rinse individual lettuce leaves to complete washing process

4 Cut off the core from the Boston lettuce and separate the leaves. Wash the leaves in plenty of cold water. Rinse each leaf under cold, running water, discard the tough stems, and tear large leaves into pieces.

5 Dry the lettuce leaves in the salad spinner or on a dish towel and add them to the large bowl.

6 Discard the tough ribs and stems from the spinach. Immerse the leaves in plenty of cold water, lifting and agitating them to loosen grit. Rinse each leaf under cold, running water.

7 Dry the spinach leaves in the salad spinner or on a dish towel and add them to the large bowl.

ANNE SAYS
"Spin small batches of leaves to extract the maximum amount of water."

9 Remove the stems from the figs and cut each fig crosswise into 4 slices, using the chef's knife.

Sweetness of fresh figs marries perfectly with savory flavor of cheese wafers

8 Strip the parsley leaves from the stems and add them to the lettuce and spinach in the bowl.

3 TOAST THE NUTS; BAKE THE WAFERS; FINISH THE SALAD

1 Heat the oven to 350°F. Spread the hazelnuts on the baking sheet and toast them in the heated oven until browned, stirring occasionally so they color evenly, 12–15 minutes. Rub the hot hazelnuts in the dish towel to remove the skins. Let cool.

Toasting loosens skin from hazelnuts

2 Using the chef's knife, coarsely chop the hazelnuts. Increase the oven heat to 400°F.

3 Cut 6 slices, about ¼-inch thick, from the dough, using the thin-bladed knife dipped in hot water.

Baked cheese wafers are very fragile so handle carefully

4 Space out the slices on the baking sheet. Re-wrap and return the remaining dough to the freezer.

ANNE SAYS
"The cheese wafers will spread during cooking, so do not worry if the slices of dough are not uniform."

5 Bake the wafers in the heated oven until they are lacy and golden brown, 6–8 minutes. Allow them to cool slightly on the baking sheet. Using the metal spatula, carefully transfer the wafers to the wire rack lined with paper towels. Allow the baking sheet to cool, slice more of the dough, and continue baking the cheese wafers as directed.

Moisten greens with dressing without soaking them

6 Divide the salad leaves and parsley among 8 individual plates. Whisk the dressing to re-emulsify it, and spoon over the greens.

🍴 **TO SERVE**
Top each serving with the chopped toasted hazelnuts. Arrange 3 cheese wafers and 3 fig slices around each salad, and top with the remaining raspberries.

V A R I A T I O N

ROASTED RED BELL PEPPER AND ARTICHOKE SALAD WITH CHEESE WAFERS

Artichoke hearts and roasted bell peppers are delicious ingredients with mixed salad leaves. Pine nuts add crunch, and balsamic vinegar provides flavor in the dressing.

1 Make the cheese wafer dough as directed in the main recipe and chill it in the freezer. Prepare the lettuces, spinach, and parsley as directed, and place in a bowl.
2 Omit the raspberries and figs. For the dressing, whisk ¼ cup balsamic vinegar with 2 tsp Dijon-style mustard, salt, and pepper. Gradually whisk in ¾ cup olive oil so the vinaigrette emulsifies and thickens.

3 Roast 3 red bell peppers: heat the broiler. Set the whole peppers on the rack about 4 inches from the heat and broil them, turning as needed, until the skin is black and blistered, 10–12 minutes. Immediately put the peppers in a plastic bag, close it, leave until cool enough to handle, then peel off the skin. Cut around each pepper core and pull it out. Halve the peppers and scrape away the seeds. Rinse under running water and pat dry. Cut each pepper half into thin strips.
4 Drain one 6-oz jar artichoke hearts packed in oil; cut them in half, or into quarters if they are large.
5 Toast ½ cup pine nuts in place of the hazelnuts. Bake the cheese wafers as directed. Add the roasted red pepper strips to the salad leaves, toss with the vinaigrette dressing, and divide the salad among 8 individual plates. Sprinkle each serving with some toasted pine nuts. Top with the artichoke hearts, and arrange the wafers on the side of each plate.

Raspberry makes pretty centerpiece for fig

Mayonnaise-based dressing is flavored with fresh raspberries and raspberry vinegar

GETTING AHEAD
The wafer dough can be prepared up to 2 days ahead and kept, tightly wrapped, in the freezer. You can make the dressing, toast the nuts, and wash the salad greens up to 1 day ahead. Refrigerate the greens, wrapped in a damp dish towel.

MIDDLE EASTERN SALADS

🍽 SERVES 6–8 🥄 WORK TIME 35–40 MINUTES*

EQUIPMENT

bowls

small knife

colander

chef's knife

citrus juicer

wooden spoons

baking sheet

strainer

chopping board

Mezze – *little dishes of vegetables, salads, olives, roasted chickpeas – form the standard opening for a meal in the Middle East. Tabbouleh – bulghur wheat with fresh mint and parsley, and cacik – yogurt and garlic with cucumber, offer contrasting textures and flavors. Pita bread is an authentic accompaniment.*

GETTING AHEAD

Both salads benefit from chilling, so make them several hours ahead and keep them, covered, in the refrigerator. Let the salads come to room temperature before serving.

*plus 2 hours chilling time

SHOPPING LIST

1 1/4 cups	bulghur wheat
2	cucumbers, total weight about 1 lb
	salt and pepper
3	garlic cloves
1	bunch of parsley
2	bunches of fresh mint
3	lemons
1 lb	medium tomatoes
3	scallions
1/2 cup	olive oil
1/2 tsp	ground coriander
1/4 tsp	ground cumin
2 cups	plain yogurt
3/4 cup	black olives for serving
6	medium pita breads for serving

INGREDIENTS

bulghur wheat

cucumbers

scallions

garlic

ground cumin

ground coriander

olive oil

tomatoes

black olives

lemons

parsley

pita bread

yogurt

mint

ANNE SAYS

"*Choose a quality, brine-cured black olive, such as the Greek Kalamata olive.*"

ORDER OF WORK

1 PREPARE THE SALAD INGREDIENTS

2 MAKE THE TABBOULEH AND CACIK

1 PREPARE THE SALAD INGREDIENTS

1 Put the bulghur wheat in a large bowl and pour over enough cold water to cover generously. Let soak, 30 minutes. Drain the bulghur wheat in the strainer. A lot of water is absorbed during soaking, so you will need to squeeze out any remaining water with your fist.

! TAKE CARE !
If the bulghur wheat is not drained sufficiently, the tabbouleh will be soggy.

Golden bulghur wheat has nutty flavor

Bulghur wheat becomes light and fluffy when soaked in water

2 Peel and trim the cucumbers and cut them lengthwise in half. Scoop out the seeds with a teaspoon. Cut each cucumber half lengthwise into 3–4 strips, then gather the strips together and cut across into dice.

3 Transfer the cucumbers to the colander, sprinkle with salt, and stir to mix. Leave them to draw out the bitter juices, 15–20 minutes.

Fragrant mint is characteristic ingredient of Middle Eastern salads

4 Meanwhile, set the flat side of the chef's knife on top of each garlic clove and strike it with your fist. Discard the skin and finely chop the garlic. Strip the parsley leaves from the stems and pile them on the chopping board. With the chef's knife, coarsely chop the leaves. Strip the mint leaves from the stems and chop the leaves.

Coarsely chopped parsley adds texture to tabbouleh

5 Squeeze the juice from the lemons; there should be about 1/2 cup juice. Discard any seeds.

6 With the tip of the small knife, cut round, remove, and discard the cores from the tomatoes.

7 Cut the tomatoes crosswise in half and squeeze out the seeds, then coarsely chop each tomato half.

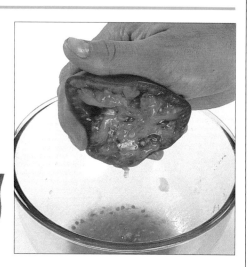

Chopped tomatoes add vivid color to tabbouleh

Sharp chef's knife chops scallions efficiently

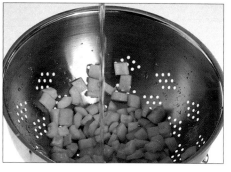

9 Rinse the juices from the diced cucumber under cold, running water. Let drain.

8 Trim and coarsely chop the scallions, including some of the green tops.

2 MAKE THE TABBOULEH AND CACIK

1 Make the tabbouleh: in a large bowl, combine the bulghur wheat, tomatoes, scallions, parsley, lemon juice, olive oil, two-thirds of the mint, and plenty of salt and pepper.

Lemon juice adds essential bite to salad

Complementary flavors and textures of tabbouleh ingredients blend after mixing

2 Mix the tabbouleh and taste for seasoning. Cover and chill in the refrigerator, at least 2 hours.

ANNE SAYS
"The proportions of bulghur wheat to fresh herbs can vary depending on your taste. More parsley or mint can be added, if you like."

3 Make the cacik: put the diced cucumbers in a bowl and add the chopped garlic, remaining mint, ground coriander, ground cumin, salt, and pepper. Pour in the yogurt.

Yogurt binds salad ingredients

4 Stir the cacik ingredients with the wooden spoon to combine, and taste for seasoning. Chill in the refrigerator, to allow flavors to blend and mellow, at least 2 hours.

¶◎¶   TO SERVE

Let the salads come to room temperature and arrange in separate bowls. Decorate the tabbouleh with olives and a mint sprig, if you like.

Cucumber is refreshing salad ingredient

Pita breads are moist, not dry, if warmed in the oven only briefly, 3–5 minutes

VARIATION

MEDITERRANEAN SALADS WITH COUSCOUS

Couscous replaces bulghur wheat in this variation of tabbouleh, while fresh dill flavors a Greek version of cacik, called tzatziki.

1 Chop 1 bunch each of fresh parsley and mint, and 1 small bunch of fresh dill. Prepare the garlic, lemon juice, tomatoes, and scallions as directed in the main recipe. Wipe, then coarsely grate 1 cucumber without peeling or seeding it. Salt and drain as directed.

2 Omit the bulghur wheat. Prepare the couscous: put $1/2$ lb couscous in a large bowl; bring 1 cup water to a boil, then pour it over the couscous, stirring quickly with a fork. Leave the couscous until plump, about 5 minutes. Finish the couscous in the same way as the tabbouleh. Taste for seasoning, cover, and chill in the refrigerator.

3 Make the tzatziki in the same way as the cacik, using the grated cucumber, with the dill in place of the mint. Taste for seasoning, cover, and chill.

4 Replace the black olives with green olives. Warm the pita bread in the oven, 3–5 minutes. Arrange the salads and olives in separate piles on 6–8 individual plates and accompany with pita bread quarters. If you like, decorate each serving with a mint sprig and a slim lemon wedge.

AUTUMN VEGETABLE SALAD

Crudités d'Automne

¶Ⓞ¶ SERVES 6 ⌣ WORK TIME 25–30 MINUTES*

EQUIPMENT

whisk

chef's knife

small knife

vegetable peeler

bowls

grater

colander

medium saucepan

shallow dish

chopping board

rubber spatula

You'll find a version of this unpretentious salad on the menu of every French bistro. A julienne of celery root in a mustard mayonnaise – céléri rémoulade – joins forces with grated carrot salad with raisins.

GETTING AHEAD

The vinaigrette dressing for the carrot salad can be made up to 1 week in advance and kept in a sealed container. The vegetables for both salads can be prepared and tossed in the dressings up to 1 day ahead; the flavors mellow on chilling.

*plus 1 hour chilling time

INGREDIENTS

celery root

Dijon-style mustard

cider vinegar

raisins

bottled mayonnaise

sugar

carrots

vegetable oil

ANNE SAYS
"*Coarsely chopped walnuts, diced apple, or toasted sunflower or pumpkin seeds, are all delicious alternatives to the raisins in the carrot salad.*"

SHOPPING LIST

	For the carrot salad and dressing
1 lb	carrots
3 tbsp	cider vinegar
1 tsp	sugar
	salt and pepper
1/3 cup	vegetable oil
1/2 cup	raisins
	For the celery root salad and dressing
1	celery root, weighing about 1 1/2 lb
3/4 cup	bottled mayonnaise
2 tbsp	Dijon-style mustard, more if needed

ORDER OF WORK

1 MAKE THE CARROT SALAD AND DRESSING

2 MAKE THE CELERY ROOT SALAD AND DRESSING

MAKE THE CARROT SALAD AND DRESSING

1 With the small knife, peel and trim the carrots. Coarsely grate them onto the shallow dish or a plate.

ANNE SAYS
"If the carrots are very young, they can be scraped rather than peeled."

Coarse side of grater yields juicy carrot shreds

Use young, sweet carrots for grating

2 In a medium bowl, whisk the vinegar with the sugar, salt, and pepper. Gradually whisk in the oil so the vinaigrette emulsifies and thickens slightly. Taste for seasoning.

3 Add the grated carrots to the vinaigrette dressing in the bowl, then add the raisins.

4 Toss together the carrots and raisins in the dressing and taste for seasoning. Cover and chill in the refrigerator, at least 1 hour.

MAKE THE CELERY ROOT SALAD AND DRESSING

3 Stack the slices, a few at a time, and cut lengthwise into very fine, even strips, guiding the knife with curled fingers.

Cut celery root strips as neatly as possible

1 Place the celery root on the chopping board and carefully slice away all the thick, knobbly peel with the chef's knife.

2 Cut a thin strip from the base of the celery root so that it lies flat on the board. Cut the celery root into thin vertical slices.

Blanching celery root keeps it white and makes it less tough

4 Put the celery root in a medium saucepan of cold, salted water, bring to a boil, and simmer the celery root until tender, 1–2 minutes.

5 Drain the celery root, rinse in cold water, and drain again thoroughly.

ANNE SAYS
"The celery root should still be crisp, but not tough."

6 In a large bowl, combine the mayonnaise, salt, pepper, and 2 tbsp mustard. Taste the dressing for seasoning, adding some more mustard to the mixture, if you like.

Creamy mayonnaise is sharpened with Dijon-style mustard

7 Add the celery root to the mustard dressing, toss, and taste for seasoning. Cover, and chill in the refrigerator, at least 1 hour.

🍴 **TO SERVE**
Arrange the celery root salad and the carrot and raisin salad side by side on individual plates.

Raisins accent the sweetness of carrots

Carrots add color to salad

VARIATION

PIQUANT BEET AND CELERY ROOT SALADS

In this version of Autumn Vegetable Salad, small cooked beets replace the carrots, and the dressing is flavored with caraway seeds. For the celery root salad, pungent fresh or bottled horseradish – a favorite in eastern France – is used instead of mustard. To serve, arrange salads attractively, in alternating curves, on a large serving plate.

1 Omit the carrots and raisins. Make the dressing as directed for carrot and raisin salad, adding 2 tsp caraway seeds with the vinegar. Wash 1 lb small beets. Do not peel or trim them before cooking because the beets "bleed."

2 Bring a saucepan of cold, salted water to a boil, add the beets and cook until tender when tested with the tip of a knife, 20–30 minutes. Drain the beets and let cool.

Skin can be easily rubbed from cooked beets

3 When the beets are cool, peel the skin from the beets with your fingers, and trim the roots and tops.

4 Coarsely grate the beets. Transfer them to the vinaigrette dressing, toss gently, and taste the salad for seasoning.

Press firmly when grating beets to make generous shreds

5 Prepare the celery root as directed. Omit the mustard. Combine the mayonnaise with 2 tbsp grated fresh or bottled horseradish, salt, and pepper. Taste for seasoning. Add the celery root. Cover both salads, and chill, at least 1 hour.

MARINATED STEAK SALAD WITH RED ONIONS

🍽 SERVES 4   🥣 WORK TIME 20–30 MINUTES*   🍲 BROILING TIME 6–12 MINUTES

EQUIPMENT

chef's knife

tongs

bowls

wooden toothpicks

non-metallic shallow dish

pastry brush

paper towels

dish towel †

whisk

chopping board

Inspired by the traditional steak sandwich, here thin strips of marinated top round are broiled with red onions and served with shredded lettuce and sliced mushrooms. The same treatment is excellent for flank steak or London broil. Crusty bread makes an ideal accompaniment.

GETTING AHEAD

The steak can be marinated up to 12 hours in the refrigerator, and the lettuce can be washed, shredded, and refrigerated, wrapped in a damp cloth. Broil the steak and onions and finish the salad just before serving.

*plus 3–12 hours marinating time

SHOPPING LIST

1 ¼ lb	top round
2	garlic cloves
1 cup	vegetable oil
3 tbsp	Worcestershire sauce
1	dash of Tabasco sauce, more to taste
	salt and pepper
1 lb	red onions
3 oz	mushrooms
1	head of red-leaf lettuce, weighing about ½ lb

INGREDIENTS

red onions

top round †

red-leaf lettuce

Tabasco sauce

garlic cloves

mushrooms

vegetable oil

Worcestershire sauce

† flank steak can also be used

ORDER OF WORK

1   **PREPARE THE MARINADE AND MARINATE THE STEAK**

2   **PREPARE THE VEGETABLES**

3   **BROIL THE STEAK AND ASSEMBLE THE SALAD**

† salad spinner can also be used

PREPARE THE MARINADE AND MARINATE THE STEAK

1 With the chef's knife, trim the meat of any fat and sinew. With the point of the knife, lightly score both sides of the meat in a lattice pattern and lay it in the shallow dish – it should be just large enough to hold the steak. Peel and chop the garlic (see box, right).

Scoring steak allows marinade to penetrate more easily

2 In a medium bowl, whisk together the oil, Worcestershire sauce, Tabasco sauce, salt, and pepper. Set aside ½ cup of this dressing for the mushrooms and finished salad. To make the marinade for the steak, add the chopped garlic to the remaining dressing and stir in with the whisk.

3 Pour the marinade over the steak. Cover, and leave to marinate in the refrigerator, turning the meat over several times, 3 hours, or up to 12 hours for maximum flavor and tenderness.

Marinade tenderizes steak

HOW TO PEEL AND CHOP GARLIC

The strength of garlic varies with its age and dryness; use more when it is very fresh.

1 To separate garlic cloves, crush a bulb with the heel of your hand, or pull a clove from the bulb with your fingers. To peel the clove, lightly crush it with the flat side of a chef's knife to loosen the skin.

2 Peel off the skin from the clove of garlic with your fingers.

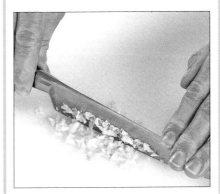

3 Set the flat side of the knife on top of the clove and strike it firmly with your fist. Finely chop the garlic with the chef's knife, moving the blade back and forth.

2 PREPARE THE VEGETABLES

1 Peel and trim the red onions. Cut a thin slice from one side of each onion, so the onions sit firmly on the chopping board. Cut the onions crosswise into ½-inch slices.

Toothpick holds onion slices together for broiling

2 Insert a wooden toothpick into the side of each onion slice to hold the slices together during cooking.

3 Wipe the mushroom caps with damp paper towels and trim the stems even with the caps. Set the mushrooms stem-side down on the chopping board and thinly slice them. Toss the mushrooms with half of the reserved dressing.

4 Twist off and discard the root end from the lettuce. Immerse the leaves in plenty of cold water, 15–30 minutes.

5 Discard the tough ribs and stems from the lettuce leaves. Dry the leaves thoroughly on the dish towel or in a salad spinner.

Pat lettuce leaves dry in dish towel

Leaves are crisp and clean after immersing in cold water

Frilly, red-edged lettuce leaves add interest to salad

Stacking leaves makes shredding lettuce quick and easy

6 Stack 5–6 of the lettuce leaves, and roll them up tightly. Coarsely shred the leaves. Stack, roll, and shred the remaining leaves and put them in a large bowl.

3 BROIL THE STEAK AND ASSEMBLE THE SALAD

Marinade moistens red onion slices while they broil

1 Heat the broiler. Using the tongs, take the steak out of the marinade, allowing the excess to drip into the dish; reserve the marinade. Lay the steak on the broiler rack. Set the onion slices around the steak.

2 Brush the onion slices with the reserved marinade in the dish. Broil the steak and onions 2–3 inches from the heat, allowing 3–4 minutes for rare meat, or 5–6 minutes for medium-done meat.

Tongs grip steak for easy turning

3 Turn over the steak and onion slices, brush with marinade, and broil the other side, 3–4 minutes for rare meat, 5–6 minutes for medium-done. Meanwhile, divide the lettuce and mushrooms among individual plates.

4 Press the steak with a finger to test if it is done: it will feel spongy if it is rare; if medium done, the steak will resist slightly when pressed.

5 Transfer the steak to the chopping board and cut it in thin diagonal slices. Arrange the steak slices on the lettuce and mushrooms.

Red onion rings add vibrant note to steak salad

6 Take the toothpicks from the onion slices, separate the rings, and arrange some over each serving.

¶⦿¶ TO SERVE
Briskly whisk the reserved dressing. Moisten each individual salad with a little of the dressing and serve at once while the steak is still warm.

Steak is mouthwateringly tender and juicy

VARIATION

ASIAN STIR-FRIED BEEF SALAD

Marinated Steak Salad travels east in this variation. Sliced raw beef soaks in a pungent marinade made spicy with hot red pepper flakes, while scallions and oriental shiitake mushrooms add flavor and color. Briskly stir-fried, served on a bed of lettuce, and topped with toasted sesame seeds, this salad is a sure winner.

6 Transfer the mushrooms and scallions to a bowl with a slotted spoon. With the slotted spoon, lift half of the meat strips from the marinade, allowing them to drain thoroughly, and add them to the hot wok or frying pan. Fry over high heat, stirring constantly, until the steak is lightly colored, 2–3 minutes. Transfer the steak strips to the bowl containing the mushrooms and scallions. With the slotted spoon, lift the remaining steak strips from the marinade and cook them in the same way as the first batch, adding more oil to the wok or frying pan if needed. Return the steak, mushrooms, and scallions in the bowl to the wok or frying pan and stir well to mix.

1 Trim the steak and cut it into ³/₈-inch diagonal slices, using a chef's knife. Cut each slice lengthwise into ³/₈-inch strips, then cut the strips across into halves or thirds. Peel and chop the garlic (see box, page 85).

2 Make the marinade as directed in the main recipe, using 3 tbsp soy sauce, and ¹/₄ tsp dried red pepper flakes in place of the Worcestershire sauce and Tabasco sauce, and whisking in only ¹/₂ cup oil with the garlic. Marinate the steak as directed, using all the marinade, 1–2 hours.

3 Toast 1 tbsp sesame seeds: heat a small frying pan over medium heat, add the seeds and toast them, stirring occasionally, until they are lightly browned, 2–3 minutes. Remove from the heat and reserve the sesame seeds to garnish the salad.

4 Omit the common mushrooms and red onions. Wipe 6 oz shiitake mushrooms, trim the stems, and thinly slice the caps. In place of fresh shiitake mushrooms, you can use 1 oz dried Chinese mushrooms: soak them in a bowl of warm water until plump, about 30 minutes, then continue as for fresh mushrooms. Trim 1 bunch scallions and cut them diagonally into 1-inch pieces, including some of the green tops. Wash and shred the lettuce as directed, and arrange it in a ring on each plate. Cut 2 limes into coronets and reserve them (see page 125).

5 Heat 1 tbsp oil in a wok or large frying pan. Add the mushrooms, scallions, salt, and pepper, and sauté over medium heat, stirring often, until they soften, 2–3 minutes.

7 Cook the steak and vegetables, stirring constantly, until very hot, about 30 seconds. Taste for seasoning, and spoon the steak strips and vegetables into the ring of lettuce on the plates. Arrange a lime coronet on each plate for squeezing, sprinkle the salad with sesame seeds, and serve warm.

PASTA AND MUSSEL SALAD

EQUIPMENT

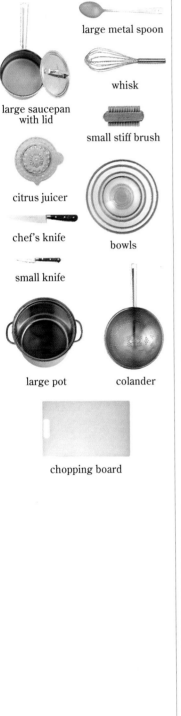

large metal spoon

whisk

small stiff brush

large saucepan with lid

citrus juicer

chef's knife

bowls

small knife

large pot

colander

chopping board

Pasta complements the texture of mussels, and generous amounts of tart dressing are absorbed by the spiral shapes, often called fusilli. Hollow shapes, such as shells and macaroni, are good too.

GETTING AHEAD
The pasta salad can be made up to 1 day ahead and refrigerated. The flavor mellows on chilling. Let the salad come to room temperature before serving. The vinaigrette dressing can be kept in a sealed container up to 1 week in the refrigerator, but do not add the shallots, garlic, or herbs until combining the mussels with the pasta.

SHOPPING LIST

2 lb	mussels
³/₄ cup	dry white wine
¹/₂ lb	pasta spirals
3	scallions
	For the herb vinaigrette dressing
4	shallots
3	garlic cloves
1	bunch of fresh tarragon
1	bunch of parsley
2	lemons
	salt and pepper
³/₄ cup	olive oil

INGREDIENTS

mussels

pasta spirals

shallots

lemons

parsley

olive oil

garlic cloves

fresh tarragon

dry white wine

scallions

ORDER OF WORK

1 MAKE THE HERB VINAIGRETTE DRESSING

2 PREPARE THE MUSSELS

3 COOK THE PASTA AND FINISH THE SALAD

1 MAKE THE HERB VINAIGRETTE DRESSING

1 Peel the shallots. Hold each one steady and slice horizontally, leaving the slices attached at the root. Slice vertically, then cut across to make fine dice. Set the flat side of the chef's knife on top of each garlic clove and strike it with your fist. Discard the skin, and finely chop the garlic.

2 Strip the tarragon and parsley leaves from the stems and pile them on the chopping board. With the chef's knife, finely chop the leaves.

Make sure your knife is very sharp to avoid bruising herbs

3 Squeeze the juice from each of the lemons; there should be about ¹/₃ cup juice altogether.

ANNE SAYS
"To extract maximum juice from lemons, roll them firmly on the work surface."

Lemon juice is used instead of vinegar in this dressing

4 Whisk together the lemon juice, half of the chopped shallots, the garlic, salt, and pepper. Gradually whisk in the oil so that the dressing emulsifies and thickens slightly. Whisk in the herbs. Taste the herb vinaigrette dressing for seasoning, and set aside.

2 PREPARE THE MUSSELS

Use back of knife blade for scraping to preserve sharp edge

1 Scrape each mussel with the small knife to remove any barnacles.

2 With the small knife, detach and discard any weed or "beard" from each mussel.

3 Scrub each one under cold, running water; discard any with broken shells or that do not close when tapped.

5 Add the mussels to the wine and shallot mixture. Cover, and cook over high heat, stirring occasionally, until the mussels open, 5–7 minutes. Transfer the mussels to a large bowl, discarding the cooking liquid. Leave until cool enough to handle.

ANNE SAYS
"Discard any mussels that have not opened at this point."

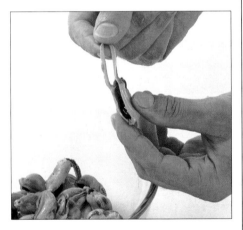

Mussels overcook quickly, so remove them from pan as soon as they are open

4 Put the wine, remaining chopped shallots, and plenty of pepper in the large saucepan. Bring to a boil and simmer, 2 minutes.

6 With your fingers, remove the mussels from their shells, reserving 4–6 mussels in their shells.

Use your fingers to pull mussel gently from its shell

7 Pull and discard the rubbery ring from around each shelled mussel, and put the mussels in a large bowl.

8 Briskly whisk the herb vinaigrette dressing. Pour the dressing over the mussels.

9 Stir gently so all the mussels are well coated with the dressing, cover, and let cool in the refrigerator while cooking the pasta.

3 COOK THE PASTA AND FINISH THE SALAD

1 Fill the large pot with water, bring to a boil, and add 1½ tsp salt. Add the pasta and simmer just until tender but still chewy, 8–10 minutes, or according to package directions. Stir occasionally to keep from sticking.

Green tops add color to salad

2 Meanwhile, trim the scallions and cut them into thin slices, including some of their green tops. Drain the pasta in the colander, rinse with cold water, and drain again thoroughly.

3 Tip the drained pasta into the bowl of mussels and dressing. Sprinkle the sliced scallions over the pasta, add salt and pepper, toss well, and taste for seasoning.

¶❂❨ TO SERVE
Arrange the pasta salad on 4–6 individual plates. Garnish each serving with a reserved mussel, adding a lemon slice and tarragon sprig, if you like.

Parsley is traditional flavoring for mussels

Mussels and pasta make mouthwatering combination

V A R I A T I O N

PASTA AND SCALLOP SALAD

The sea scallops in this variation are tossed in a creamy herb dressing and served with spinach pasta.

1 Omit the mussels and white wine. Chop the garlic, 2 shallots only, the fresh tarragon, and parsley as directed. Chop 1 bunch of fresh chives. Make the dressing as directed, using half of the chopped garlic, 1 lemon only, and ½ cup olive oil. Whisk in the herbs with 3 tbsp heavy cream, and taste for seasoning.

2 Prepare 1 lb sea scallops in place of the mussels: if necessary, discard the tough, crescent-shaped membrane at the side of each scallop. Rinse the scallops with cold water, drain, and pat dry. Cut large scallops into 2 rounds. Heat 1 tbsp olive oil in a large frying pan to very hot. Add the scallops with the remaining garlic, and sprinkle them with salt and pepper. Sauté, turning once, until brown and slightly crisp, 1–2 minutes on each side. If the scallops are small, shake the pan so they color evenly on all sides, rather than turn them.

3 Cook ½ lb spinach pasta and slice the scallions as directed. Drain the pasta. Toss with the scallions, scallops, and creamy herb dressing. Taste for seasoning and serve at room temperature. Garnish each serving with chives, if you like.

Lentil Salad with Knackwurst

¶◉¶ Serves 4 · Work Time 30–35 minutes* · Cooking Time 45–55 minutes

Equipment

saucepans, 1 with lid

chef's knife

bowls

whisk

vegetable peeler

slotted spoon

wooden spoon

kitchen string

metal skewer

chopping board

In this hearty winter salad, lentils are tossed in an herb and mustard vinaigrette dressing, and served with slices of hot sausage.

Getting Ahead

The dressing can be made up to 1 week in advance and kept in a sealed container; do not add the herbs until just before serving. The lentils can be cooked and tossed with dressing up to 1 day ahead, and kept, covered, in the refrigerator.

*plus 1 hour chilling time

Shopping List

3	garlic cloves
1	large onion
1	celery stalk
2 tbsp	vegetable oil
1½ cups	lentils
1	bouquet garni (see box, page 95)
3 cups	chicken stock (see box, page 96) or water, more if needed
	salt and pepper
1 lb	knackwurst
	For the herb vinaigrette dressing
10–12	sprigs of fresh thyme
1	bunch of fresh chives
¼ cup	cider vinegar
2 tsp	Dijon-style mustard
1 tsp	mustard powder
⅔ cup	vegetable oil

Ingredients

lentils

knackwurst †

garlic cloves

vegetable oil

fresh thyme

celery stalk

bouquet garni

chicken stock

Dijon-style mustard

cider vinegar

fresh chives

onion

mustard powder

†kielbasa sausage can also be used

Order of Work

1 Cook the Lentils and Make the Herb Vinaigrette Dressing

2 Cook the Knackwurst and Finish the Salad

1 COOK THE LENTILS AND MAKE THE HERB VINAIGRETTE DRESSING

1 Set the flat side of the chef's knife on top of each garlic clove; strike it with your fist. Discard the skin and finely chop the garlic. Peel the onion, leaving a little of the root attached, and cut lengthwise in half. Slice each half horizontally toward the root, then vertically. Cut across to make dice.

ANNE SAYS
"Green lentils are used here, but orange lentils are good, too."

Green lentils hold their shape during cooking

2 Peel the strings from the celery stalk. Cut the stalk across into thin slices. Heat the oil in a medium saucepan. Add the chopped onion and celery, and sauté, stirring occasionally, until soft but not brown, 2–3 minutes. Add the garlic to the onion and celery, and cook 1 minute longer.

3 Add the lentils to the vegetables and tie the bouquet garni to the saucepan handle. Pour in the chicken stock or water, season with salt and pepper, and cover the pan. Simmer the lentils until tender, stirring occasionally, 25–30 minutes.

ANNE SAYS
"If the lentils seem dry during cooking, add more stock or water."

HOW TO MAKE A BOUQUET GARNI

This bundle of aromatic flavoring herbs is designed to be easily lifted from the casserole or saucepan and discarded at the end of cooking.

To make a bouquet garni, hold together 5–6 parsley stems, 2–3 sprigs of fresh thyme, and 1 bay leaf. Wind a piece of string around the herbs and tie securely, leaving a length of string to tie to the casserole or saucepan handle, if necessary.

Hold herbs firmly together and tie into neat bouquet with string

4 At the end of cooking, the lentils should have absorbed all the liquid. Discard the bouquet garni.

5 Make the herb vinaigrette dressing: strip the thyme leaves from some of the stems, reserving 4 sprigs for decoration. With the chef's knife, chop two-thirds of the chives. Cut the remaining chives into ³/₄-inch pieces and reserve for decoration.

6 In a small bowl, whisk together the vinegar, mustard, mustard powder, salt, and pepper. Gradually whisk in the oil so the vinaigrette dressing emulsifies and thickens slightly.

7 Add the thyme leaves and chopped chives, and taste for seasoning. Briskly whisk the vinaigrette.

CHICKEN STOCK

Chicken stock is an indispensable ingredient in many recipes. The longer it simmers, the more flavor it has. Because it is often reduced to concentrate, salt is not usually added while stock is cooking. Whole peppercorns should be used rather than ground pepper, because ground pepper can turn bitter with prolonged cooking. Homemade chicken stock keeps up to 3 days, in a covered container, in the refrigerator. Chicken stock also freezes well.

🍽️ MAKES ABOUT 2 QUARTS

🥄 WORK TIME 15 MINUTES

🍲 COOKING TIME UP TO 3 HOURS

SHOPPING LIST

1	stewing chicken
1	onion, quartered
1	carrot, quartered
1	celery stalk, quartered
1	bouquet garni, made with 5–6 parsley stems, 2–3 sprigs of fresh thyme, and 1 bay leaf
¹/₂–1 tsp	peppercorns
2 quarts	water, more if needed

1 Put the ingredients in a large pot, with water to cover. Bring to a boil, and simmer until the chicken thighs are tender, skimming the stock occasionally, 1¹/₄–1¹/₂ hours.

2 Remove the chicken from the stock. Continue simmering the stock, about 1¹/₂ hours. Using a ladle, strain the stock into a large bowl.

8 Transfer the cooked lentils and vegetables to a bowl, and let cool slightly. Pour the herb vinaigrette dressing over the lentils. Gently mix the salad with the wooden spoon until the lentils are well coated with the dressing. Taste for seasoning, then cover, and chill in the refrigerator, at least 1 hour.

Herbs and mustard in dressing enhance flavor of lentils

Add dressing to lentils while they are still warm so that they absorb maximum amount

2 COOK THE KNACKWURST AND FINISH THE SALAD

1 Prick the sausages, and put in a pan with water to cover. Bring just to a boil, reduce the heat, and simmer very gently, until the skewer inserted in one of them is warm when withdrawn, 20–25 minutes. Meanwhile, let the salad come to room temperature.

Prick sausages so skins do not split

2 With the slotted spoon, transfer the sausages to the chopping board and cut them crosswise into ½-inch diagonal slices.

❡◉❡ TO SERVE

Divide the lentil salad among 4 plates and add the sausage slices. Decorate with the reserved chives and thyme sprigs, and serve while the sausage slices are warm.

Lightly smoked sausage combines well with earthy taste of lentils

Lentils help create a salad of substance

V A R I A T I O N

WHITE BEANS WITH SALAMI

Here, spicy Italian sausage and flat-leaf parsley enliven white kidney beans.

1 Omit the lentils and knackwurst. Put 1½ cups dried white kidney beans in a large bowl. Add water to cover them generously, and leave them to soak overnight. Drain the beans, rinse with cold water, and drain again.

2 Chop the onion, 5 garlic cloves, and celery. Sauté them as directed in the main recipe, reserving one-third of the chopped garlic for the dressing. Add the beans, chicken stock or water, and bouquet garni, and simmer, covered, just until tender, 1–1½ hours. Do not add salt until halfway through cooking, or the skins of the beans will be tough. Drain off any excess liquid.

3 Omit the herb vinaigrette dressing. Whisk together ¼ cup red wine vinegar, the reserved garlic, salt, and pepper. Gradually whisk in ⅔ cup olive oil. Taste for seasoning.

4 In a large bowl, gently combine the kidney beans and dressing, and taste for seasoning. Cover, and chill in the refrigerator, 1 hour. Coarsely chop 1 small bunch of flat-leaf parsley, reserving 4 sprigs for decoration.

5 To finish: let the salad come to room temperature. Trim the rind from ½ lb spicy Italian-style salami, cut it into ⅜-inch slices, then into dice. Stir the chopped parsley into the salad and divide it among 4 individual plates. Add the diced salami, and accompany each serving with a parsley sprig.

ASIAN NOODLE SALAD

EQUIPMENT

chef's knife

small knife

large pot

whisk

medium saucepan

bowls

colander

chopping board

rubber gloves

large forks

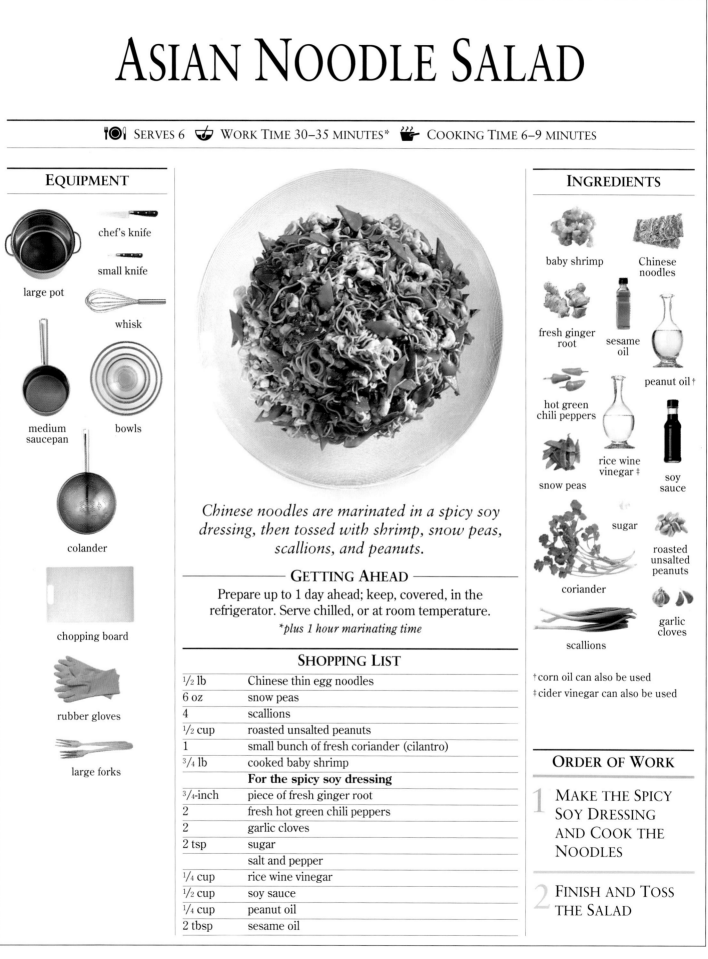

Chinese noodles are marinated in a spicy soy dressing, then tossed with shrimp, snow peas, scallions, and peanuts.

GETTING AHEAD

Prepare up to 1 day ahead; keep, covered, in the refrigerator. Serve chilled, or at room temperature.

*plus 1 hour marinating time

SHOPPING LIST

½ lb	Chinese thin egg noodles
6 oz	snow peas
4	scallions
½ cup	roasted unsalted peanuts
1	small bunch of fresh coriander (cilantro)
¾ lb	cooked baby shrimp
	For the spicy soy dressing
¾-inch	piece of fresh ginger root
2	fresh hot green chili peppers
2	garlic cloves
2 tsp	sugar
	salt and pepper
¼ cup	rice wine vinegar
½ cup	soy sauce
¼ cup	peanut oil
2 tbsp	sesame oil

INGREDIENTS

baby shrimp

Chinese noodles

fresh ginger root

sesame oil

peanut oil †

hot green chili peppers

rice wine vinegar ‡

soy sauce

snow peas

sugar

roasted unsalted peanuts

coriander

scallions

garlic cloves

† corn oil can also be used
‡ cider vinegar can also be used

ORDER OF WORK

1 MAKE THE SPICY SOY DRESSING AND COOK THE NOODLES

2 FINISH AND TOSS THE SALAD

1 MAKE THE SPICY SOY DRESSING AND COOK THE NOODLES

1 With the small knife, peel the skin from the ginger root. With the chef's knife, slice the ginger, cutting across the fibrous grain. Crush each slice with the flat of the knife, then finely chop the slices.

2 Core, seed, and dice the fresh hot chili peppers (see box, page 100). Set the flat side of the chef's knife on top of each garlic clove and strike it with your fist. Discard the skin and finely chop the garlic.

3 Put the ginger, hot chili peppers, garlic, sugar, pepper, and vinegar in a bowl. Pour in the soy sauce.

4 Gradually whisk in the peanut and sesame oils so the sauce emulsifies and thickens slightly. Taste the dressing for seasoning.

Sesame oil adds nutty flavor to dressing

Whisk as you pour in peanut oil

5 Fill the large pot with water, bring to a boil, and add salt. Add the noodles and simmer just until they are tender but still chewy, 4–6 minutes, or according to package directions. Stir them occasionally to prevent sticking.

7 Transfer the noodles to a large bowl. Briskly whisk the dressing, pour it over the noodles, and toss until well coated. Set aside to marinate, at least 1 hour for the flavor to mellow.

ANNE SAYS
"Toss the noodles while warm; they will absorb more flavor."

6 Drain the noodles in the colander, rinse with hot water, and drain again thoroughly.

Large forks are useful for tossing noodles in dressing

HOW TO CORE, SEED, AND DICE A FRESH HOT CHILI PEPPER

Fresh hot chili peppers, such as jalapeños, must be finely chopped so heat is spread evenly through the dish. Be sure to wear rubber gloves and to avoid contact with eyes because hot chili peppers can burn your hands and eyes.

1 Cut the chili pepper lengthwise in half. Cut out the core, scrape out the seeds, and cut away the fleshy white ribs.

2 Set each half cut-side up on a chopping board and cut it lengthwise into very thin strips.

3 Gather the strips together and cut across into very fine dice with a small knife.

2 FINISH AND TOSS THE SALAD

Pull strings from snow peas so they are not tough when cooked

1 Meanwhile, trim the stem end from each snow pea and pull the string down the pod. Trim the other end.

2 Cook the snow peas in boiling salted water until tender but still crisp, 2–3 minutes. Drain, rinse with cold water, and drain again. Stack a few pods at a time and cut across diagonally into 2–3 slices.

3 Using the chef's knife, trim the scallions and cut them crosswise into thin diagonal slices, including some of the green tops.

4 With the chef's knife, coarsely chop the peanuts. Strip the coriander leaves from the stems, pile the leaves on the chopping board, and coarsely chop them.

Toss salad so ingredients are well coated in savory dressing

5 Add the snow peas, scallions, two-thirds of both the chopped peanuts and coriander, and all of the shrimp to the noodles. Toss the salad ingredients thoroughly. Taste for seasoning. It may be unnecessary to add salt because soy sauce is salty.

¶◉¶ TO SERVE
Mound the salad onto a serving plate and top with the remaining chopped peanuts and coriander.

Chopped coriander preserves its bright color when added to salad at last moment

Baby shrimp are full of flavor

V A R I A T I O N

THAI NOODLE SALAD

In this recipe, sliced pork replaces the shrimp and the dressing includes Thai flavorings of lemon grass and lime juice. It is a great way to use up leftover pork.

1 Make the dressing: omit the ginger and rice wine vinegar. Chop the garlic and hot chili peppers. Coarsely chop 1 stalk of lemon grass and squeeze the juice from 1 lime. Whisk together the soy sauce, lime juice, garlic, chili peppers, lemon grass, sugar, and pepper. Gradually whisk in the oils. Taste the dressing for seasoning.

2 Cook and drain the noodles as directed in the main recipe and toss them in the dressing.

3 Omit the shrimp and snow peas. Cut 1/2 lb cooked pork into thin slices. Stack the slices and cut them into 1/8-inch strips.

4 Chop the peanuts and fresh coriander. Coarsely chop 7–10 sprigs of fresh basil. Drain an 8-oz can of sliced water chestnuts.

5 Toss the noodles and dressing with the sliced pork, water chestnuts, scallions, all of the chopped peanuts, and the herbs. Cover, and let stand, at least 1 hour.

6 Divide the salad among 6 individual plates. Garnish each serving with a basil sprig, if you like.

SALADE NIÇOISE

🍽 SERVES 6 ⤵ WORK TIME 25–30 MINUTES 🍲 COOKING TIME 15–20 MINUTES

EQUIPMENT

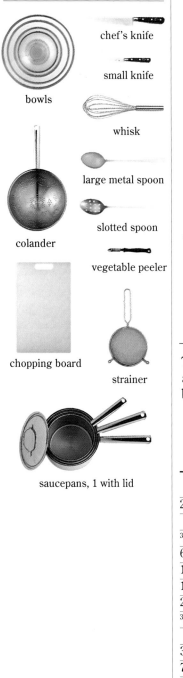

chef's knife

small knife

whisk

large metal spoon

slotted spoon

vegetable peeler

bowls

colander

chopping board

strainer

saucepans, 1 with lid

INGREDIENTS

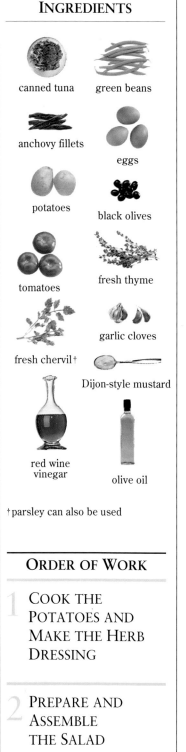

canned tuna

green beans

anchovy fillets

eggs

potatoes

black olives

tomatoes

fresh thyme

fresh chervil†

garlic cloves

Dijon-style mustard

red wine vinegar

olive oil

†parsley can also be used

This salad is from Nice in southern France, home town of the great French chef, Escoffier, who wrote various recipes for it. This version is complete with potatoes, green beans, eggs, tomatoes, anchovies, and canned tuna.

GETTING AHEAD

The dressing can be made up to 1 week ahead and stored in a sealed container; do not add the garlic and herbs until just before using. The eggs can be hard-boiled 1 day ahead. Shell, and keep them refrigerated in cold water. Prepare other ingredients up to 6 hours ahead. Add the dressing to the beans and assemble the salad not more than 1 hour ahead.

SHOPPING LIST

2 lb	potatoes
	salt and pepper
³⁄₄ lb	green beans
6	eggs
1 lb	medium tomatoes
10	anchovy fillets
2	6¹⁄₂-oz cans solid light tuna
³⁄₄ cup	black olives
	For the herb vinaigrette dressing
3	garlic cloves
7–10	sprigs of fresh thyme
1	bunch of fresh chervil
¹⁄₂ cup	red wine vinegar
2 tsp	Dijon-style mustard
1¹⁄₂ cups	olive oil

ORDER OF WORK

1 COOK THE POTATOES AND MAKE THE HERB DRESSING

2 PREPARE AND ASSEMBLE THE SALAD

1 COOK THE POTATOES AND MAKE THE HERB DRESSING

Sharp knife ensures chervil is not bruised when cutting

Thyme adds Mediterranean flavor

1 Peel the potatoes and, if using large ones, cut into 2–4 pieces. Put them in a large saucepan of cold, salted water, cover, and bring to a boil. Simmer just until tender when pierced with the tip of a knife, 15–20 minutes.

2 Meanwhile, make the vinaigrette: peel and finely chop the garlic cloves. Strip the thyme and chervil leaves from the stems. With the chef's knife, finely chop the chervil leaves.

3 In a bowl, whisk the wine vinegar with the mustard, chopped garlic, salt, and pepper. Slowly whisk in the olive oil so the dressing emulsifies and thickens slightly.

Pour oil into dressing in a slow, steady stream, whisking constantly with your other hand

Dressing starts to thicken slightly

4 Add the thyme and chopped chervil to the vinaigrette, whisk well to mix the ingredients together, and taste for seasoning.

5 Drain the potatoes, rinse with warm water, and drain again thoroughly. Cut the potatoes into chunks and put them in a large bowl.

6 Briskly whisk the herb vinaigrette. Spoon 5–6 tbsp over the potatoes – they will absorb more dressing when warm. Stir with the large metal spoon so that the potatoes are thoroughly coated. Taste for seasoning. Let cool.

2 PREPARE AND ASSEMBLE THE SALAD

Flavor will improve if green beans are marinated in dressing up to half an hour

Be sure to taste beans for seasoning after adding dressing

1 Top and tail the beans. Bring a saucepan of salted water to a boil. Add the beans and cook until tender but still firm, 5–7 minutes. Drain, rinse with cold water, and drain again.

2 Put the beans in a bowl. Briskly whisk the remaining vinaigrette dressing and add 3–4 tbsp to the beans. Toss them so they are thoroughly coated in dressing. Taste for seasoning.

Egg wedges will team up with tomato wedges for colorful presentation

3 Put the eggs in a pan of cold water, bring to a boil, and simmer, 10 minutes. Transfer to cold water. Let cool, and drain. Crack and remove the shells; rinse the eggs with cold water. Cut each egg lengthwise into quarters.

4 Peel the tomatoes (see box, below). Cut the tomatoes in half. Slice each half into 4 wedges. Drain the anchovies. Drain the tuna; put it in a bowl.

HOW TO PEEL TOMATOES

1 Bring a small saucepan of water to a boil. Cut the cores from the tomatoes and score an "x" on the base of each tomato with the tip of a small knife.

2 Immerse the tomatoes in the boiling water until the skins start to split, 8–15 seconds, depending on their ripeness. Transfer them at once to a bowl of cold water.

3 When the tomatoes are cool, peel off the skins with the help of the small knife.

5 Flake the tuna with a fork. Briskly whisk the vinaigrette dressing, then stir 5–6 tbsp into the tuna.

6 Arrange the potatoes in a large, shallow serving bowl. Put the green beans in the center, then spoon the tuna on top.

Each ingredient for this salad is always arranged individually, not tossed with others

7 Alternate a few egg and tomato wedges on the tuna and the remaining wedges around the edge of the bowl. Briskly whisk the remaining dressing and spoon it over the salad.

🍽 TO SERVE

Arrange the olives and crosses of 2 anchovy fillets inside the egg and tomato border. Serve the salad at room temperature.

Anchovies give salty flavor to this salad

1 Immerse 6 bamboo skewers in water in a shallow dish and set aside to soak, 30 minutes. Alternatively, use metal skewers which do not need to be soaked. Make the herb vinaigrette dressing as directed in the main recipe.

2 Core the tomatoes and cut them into wedges. Omit the canned tuna. Cut 2 lb fresh tuna into 1-inch cubes and thread the cubes onto the skewers, alternating them with the tomato wedges. Transfer the kebabs to a shallow non-metallic dish. Briskly whisk the herb vinaigrette dressing and pour 5–6 tbsp over the kebabs. Cover and marinate in the refrigerator, turning the skewers occasionally, 1 hour.

3 Meanwhile, prepare the remaining salad ingredients as directed and arrange them on individual plates.

4 Heat the broiler and oil the broiler rack. Transfer the kebabs to the rack, reserving the marinade for basting. Season the tuna with salt and pepper. Broil the kebabs about 3 inches from the heat, 2 minutes. Turn the skewers, baste the tuna and tomatoes with the reserved marinade, and broil until the tuna is lightly browned on the outside and still slightly rare in the center, about 2 minutes longer. Transfer the kebabs to the salads, pour over the remaining dressing, and serve immediately.

WALDORF CHICKEN SALAD

¶O¶ SERVES 6 · WORK TIME 25–30 MINUTES* · COOKING TIME 25–35 MINUTES

EQUIPMENT

- chef's knife
- small knife
- vegetable peeler
- melon baller ‡
- wide shallow pan †
- paper towels
- bowls
- slotted spoon
- wooden spoon
- chopping board
- tongs
- baking sheet

† shallow saucepan can also be used

‡ teaspoon can also be used

INGREDIENTS

- apples
- chicken breast halves
- walnuts
- plain yogurt
- bouquet garni
- bottled mayonnaise
- lemon
- carrot
- black peppercorns
- onion
- celery

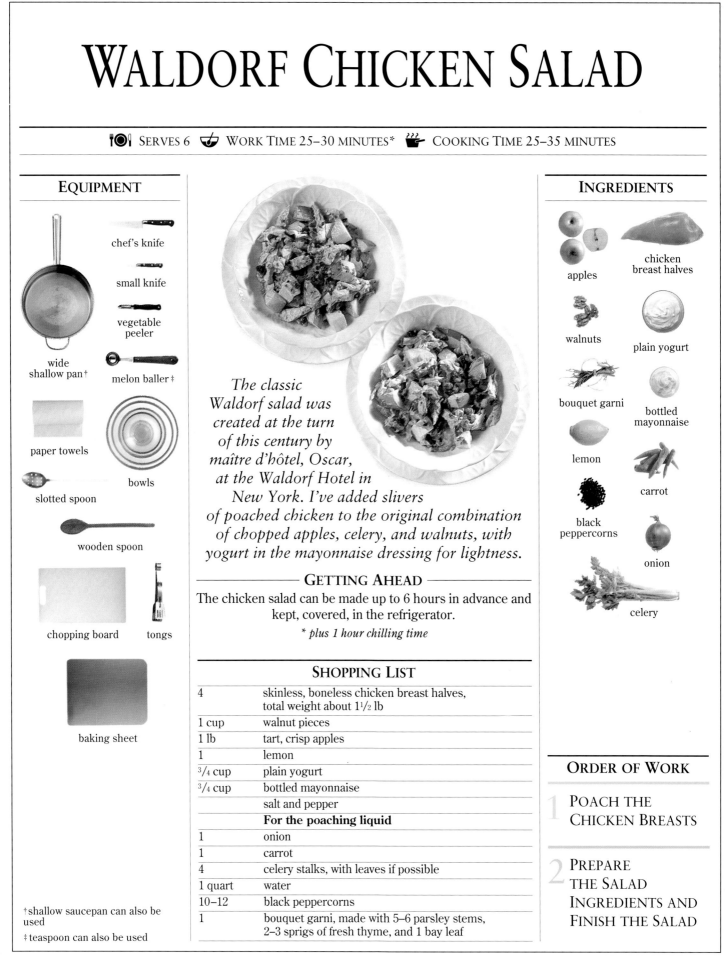

The classic Waldorf salad was created at the turn of this century by maître d'hôtel, Oscar, at the Waldorf Hotel in New York. I've added slivers of poached chicken to the original combination of chopped apples, celery, and walnuts, with yogurt in the mayonnaise dressing for lightness.

GETTING AHEAD
The chicken salad can be made up to 6 hours in advance and kept, covered, in the refrigerator.

* plus 1 hour chilling time

SHOPPING LIST

4	skinless, boneless chicken breast halves, total weight about 1¹/₂ lb
1 cup	walnut pieces
1 lb	tart, crisp apples
1	lemon
³/₄ cup	plain yogurt
³/₄ cup	bottled mayonnaise
	salt and pepper
	For the poaching liquid
1	onion
1	carrot
4	celery stalks, with leaves if possible
1 quart	water
10–12	black peppercorns
1	bouquet garni, made with 5–6 parsley stems, 2–3 sprigs of fresh thyme, and 1 bay leaf

ORDER OF WORK

1 POACH THE CHICKEN BREASTS

2 PREPARE THE SALAD INGREDIENTS AND FINISH THE SALAD

1 POACH THE CHICKEN BREASTS

1 Trim and peel the onion and carrot, and cut them into quarters. Gather the celery stalks together, and trim off the tops and leaves, setting the stalks aside for the salad.

Bouquet garni completes flavorings for poaching liquid

Celery tops and leaves, with carrot and onion, add flavor to chicken poaching liquid

2 Pour the water into the wide shallow pan. Add the peppercorns, onion and carrot quarters, celery tops and leaves, bouquet garni, and salt. Bring to a boil and simmer, 10–15 minutes.

3 Meanwhile, strip the tendon from the underside of each chicken breast, stroking it with a knife to remove it cleanly. The small piece of fillet meat will also be loosened.

4 Add the chicken to the poaching liquid, and simmer until the juices run clear, not pink, when the meat is pierced at the thickest portion, 5–8 minutes for the fillets, 10–12 minutes for the breasts, turning them once.

5 Remove from the heat. Return the cooked fillets to cool in the poaching liquid with the chicken breasts, 10–15 minutes. Transfer the chicken breasts and fillets to paper towels to drain.

Cooling chicken in poaching liquid keeps flesh moist

6 With your fingers, pull the chicken breasts into slivers about 2 inches long. Divide the fillets in half. The meat is juicier if you do not cut across the fibers with a knife.

2 PREPARE THE SALAD INGREDIENTS AND FINISH THE SALAD

1 Heat the oven to 350°F. Spread the walnut pieces on the baking sheet and bake them in the heated oven until crisp, stirring occasionally so that they toast evenly, 5–8 minutes.

2 Peel the strings from each of the celery stalks with the vegetable peeler. Cut the celery stalks crosswise at an angle into 1/4-inch slices.

Melon baller scoops out apple cores efficiently but a sharp-edged teaspoon can also be used

3 With the small knife, cut the flower and stem ends from each of the apples, but do not peel them. Cut the apples in half and scoop out the cores, using the melon baller.

4 Lay each apple half flat on the chopping board. Cut horizontally in half, then cut vertically into 3/8-inch slices. Gather the slices together and cut crosswise to make dice. Transfer the apples to a large bowl.

6 Add the chicken, celery, yogurt, mayonnaise, and two-thirds of the walnut pieces to the apple. Season with salt and pepper.

Yogurt lightens traditional mayonnaise dressing for Waldorf salad

Apples coated in lemon juice do not discolor

5 Cut the lemon in half and squeeze the juice over the diced apples. Stir with the wooden spoon so that the apples are thoroughly coated.

7 Stir the ingredients together until combined. Taste for seasoning, cover, and chill, 1 hour.

8 Coarsely chop the remaining walnut pieces and set aside to garnish the individual salad servings.

VARIATION

TROPICAL CHICKEN SALAD

Waldorf chicken salad takes on an exotic flavor in this recipe, with the addition of cumin, cardamom, coriander, and tropical fruit. I suggest papaya and mango to set off the pale green of the melon balls. You could also include star fruit, kiwi fruit, or pomegranate seeds.

1 Prepare and poach the chicken breast halves as directed in the main recipe. Omit the toasted walnuts, apples, celery, and mayonnaise.

2 Halve 1 small honeydew, or other green-fleshed melon, weighing about 1 lb. Scoop out and discard the seeds from the melon. With a melon baller, cut balls from the melon flesh into a large bowl.

3 Halve 1 medium papaya, weighing about 1/2 lb. Scoop out and discard the dark seeds from the center. Cut balls from the papaya flesh into the bowl.

4 Cut 1 medium mango (weighing about 3/4 lb) lengthwise into 2 pieces, slightly off-center so that the knife just misses the pit. Repeat on the other side of the fruit, leaving a thin layer of flesh around the pit. With a small knife, slash one half of the mango in a lattice at 1/2-inch intervals, cutting through the flesh but not the peel.

Tart apples contribute color and flavor

Chicken is tender and juicy

¡©¡ TO SERVE
Transfer the chilled salad to individual bowls, sprinkle the chopped walnuts over the top, and serve.

5 Holding the mango flesh upward, carefully push the center of the peel with your thumbs to turn it inside out. Cut the flesh away from the skin into the bowl. Repeat with the other half.

6 Add the chicken to the fruit. Combine 1 cup plain yogurt, juice of 1 lemon, pepper, and 1/4 tsp each ground cumin, ground cardamom, and ground coriander. Season with salt, and taste. Add the dressing to the salad and stir to combine. Taste, and chill.

7 Transfer the salad to a large serving platter. Decorate with lemon twists and mint sprigs, if you like.

WARM SALMON, ORANGE, AND LAMB'S LETTUCE SALAD

🍽️ SERVES 6   🥣 WORK TIME 35–40 MINUTES   🍲 COOKING TIME 6–12 MINUTES

EQUIPMENT

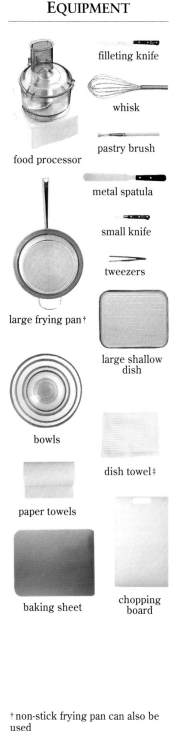

- filleting knife
- whisk
- pastry brush
- food processor
- metal spatula
- small knife
- tweezers
- large frying pan†
- large shallow dish
- bowls
- dish towel‡
- paper towels
- baking sheet
- chopping board

†non-stick frying pan can also be used
‡salad spinner can also be used

INGREDIENTS

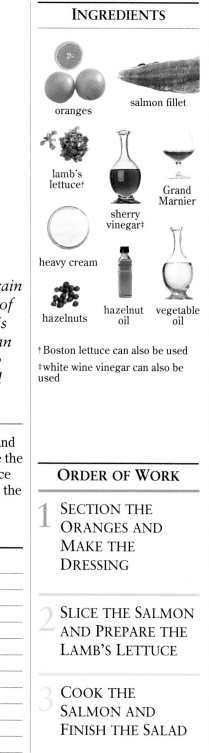

- oranges
- salmon fillet
- lamb's lettuce†
- sherry vinegar‡
- Grand Marnier
- heavy cream
- hazelnuts
- hazelnut oil
- vegetable oil

† Boston lettuce can also be used
‡ white wine vinegar can also be used

At our home in Burgundy, with the wind and rain of October, come the first treasured bunches of mâche, which flourishes in the garden. In this recipe, the velvety lamb's lettuce is tossed in an orange and hazelnut dressing, enriched with cream and Grand Marnier, to provide a bed for salmon slices.

GETTING AHEAD

The oranges can be sectioned, the dressing prepared, and the lamb's lettuce washed, up to 1 day ahead. Refrigerate the orange sections in a covered bowl and the lamb's lettuce wrapped in a damp dish towel. Cook the salmon and add the nuts to the dressing just before serving.

SHOPPING LIST

1 lb	salmon fillet
½ lb	lamb's lettuce (mâche)
1 tbsp	vegetable oil
	For the orange and hazelnut dressing
4	oranges
¼ cup	hazelnuts
	salt and pepper
2 tbsp	sherry vinegar
1 tbsp	Grand Marnier
2 tbsp	heavy cream
½ cup	hazelnut oil

ORDER OF WORK

1   SECTION THE ORANGES AND MAKE THE DRESSING

2   SLICE THE SALMON AND PREPARE THE LAMB'S LETTUCE

3   COOK THE SALMON AND FINISH THE SALAD

1 SECTION THE ORANGES AND MAKE THE DRESSING

2 Heat the oven to 350°F. Spread the hazelnuts on the baking sheet and toast until lightly browned, stirring occasionally, 12–15 minutes. Rub the hot hazelnuts in the dish towel to remove the skins, then let cool.

! TAKE CARE !
The longer nuts are toasted, the stronger the flavor. Do not over-toast or they will be bitter.

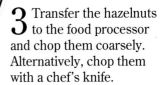

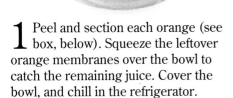

1 Peel and section each orange (see box, below). Squeeze the leftover orange membranes over the bowl to catch the remaining juice. Cover the bowl, and chill in the refrigerator.

3 Transfer the hazelnuts to the food processor and chop them coarsely. Alternatively, chop them with a chef's knife.

HOW TO PEEL AND SECTION A CITRUS FRUIT

Citrus fruit flesh is often cut into sections for salads. The technique is the same for any citrus fruit. Seedless fruit, such as navel oranges, are best for sectioning.

Hold orange over bowl to catch juice and sections

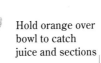

1 Cut away both ends of the fruit just to the flesh. Set the fruit upright on a chopping board. Working from top to bottom, cut away the zest, pith, and skin, following the curve of the fruit.

2 Working over a bowl to catch the juice, hold the fruit in your hand and slide a knife down one side of a section, cutting it away from the membrane. Cut down the other side and release the section into the bowl.

3 Continue cutting, folding back the membranes like the pages of a book, discarding any seeds.

4 Transfer 3 tbsp juice from the oranges to another bowl. Add salt, and pepper, vinegar, Grand Marnier, and heavy cream; whisk together.

5 Gradually whisk in all but 2 tbsp of the hazelnut oil, so that the dressing emulsifies and thickens slightly. Add the hazelnuts to the dressing, whisk them in, and taste for seasoning.

2 SLICE THE SALMON AND PREPARE THE LAMB'S LETTUCE

1 Rinse the salmon fillet with cold water. Pat dry with paper towels.

Rinse salmon before slicing

2 Using the filleting knife, trim off any cartilage from the salmon. If necessary, pull out any pin bones with the tweezers.

3 Holding the fish steady with one hand, with the tail facing away from you, and working toward it, use the filleting knife to cut 12 slices, about 1/4-inch thick. Keep the slices as even as possible, leaving any skin behind.

Lamb's lettuce can be gritty, so immerse leaves in cold water to loosen dirt

Lift lamb's lettuce from water with your hands, leaving grit at bottom of bowl

4 Wash the lamb's lettuce in plenty of cold water and pinch away any root ends, keeping the small bunches of leaves intact. Dry the lamb's lettuce on the dish towel or in a salad spinner.

3 COOK THE SALMON AND FINISH THE SALAD

1 Toss the lamb's lettuce with half of the dressing and taste for seasoning. Arrange on 6 individual plates. Heat the 1 tbsp vegetable oil in the frying pan. Sprinkle the salmon slices with salt and pepper. Cook a batch of salmon slices in the heated frying pan over high heat until lightly browned, 1–2 minutes each side.

! TAKE CARE !
Do not overcook the salmon slices or they will fall apart.

3 With the metal spatula, add 2 warm salmon slices to each plate of dressed lamb's lettuce.

2 Transfer the slices to the dish and cook the remaining salmon slices, adding each batch to the dish. Brush the salmon with 2 tbsp of the juice from the oranges and the 2 tbsp hazelnut oil.

¶◎¶ TO SERVE
Arrange the orange sections on the lamb's lettuce. Divide the remaining dressing between the servings, spooning a cluster of hazelnuts on the salmon. Serve at once.

Warm salmon contrasts with cool lamb's lettuce

VARIATION

WARM MONKFISH SALAD WITH HORSERADISH
Monkfish slices, topped with a cool, creamy horseradish dressing star in this salad.

1 Omit the oranges and orange and hazelnut dressing. Prepare the lamb's lettuce as directed. Make the horseradish dressing: squeeze the juice from 1/2 lemon. In a small bowl, whisk together 2 tbsp sherry vinegar, the lemon juice, 3 tbsp grated fresh or bottled horseradish, salt, and pepper. Gradually whisk in 3/4 cup peanut or corn oil so the dressing emulsifies and thickens slightly. Taste for seasoning, and chill in the refrigerator. Trim and thinly slice 6 large red radishes.

2 Substitute 1 lb monkfish fillets for the salmon fillet. If necessary, cut away the thin membrane that covers the flesh of monkfish. Rinse the fillets in cold water, pat dry, and cut into slices 1/4-inch thick.

3 Sauté the monkfish slices in batches, in the same way as the salmon, 2–3 minutes each side. Toss the lamb's lettuce with half of the dressing and taste for seasoning. Divide it among 6 plates. Whisk 3 tbsp heavy cream into the remaining dressing. Set 3 monkfish slices in the center of each serving. Spoon the dressing over the top, and circle with the radish slices.

LACQUERED CHICKEN SALAD

🍽 SERVES 4   🥣 WORK TIME 25–30 MINUTES*   ♨ BROILING TIME 10–15 MINUTES

EQUIPMENT

chef's knife

small knife

shallow
non-metallic
dish

pastry brush

whisk

salad spinner†

bowls

strainer

tongs

chopping board

broiler pan and rack

† dish towel can also be used

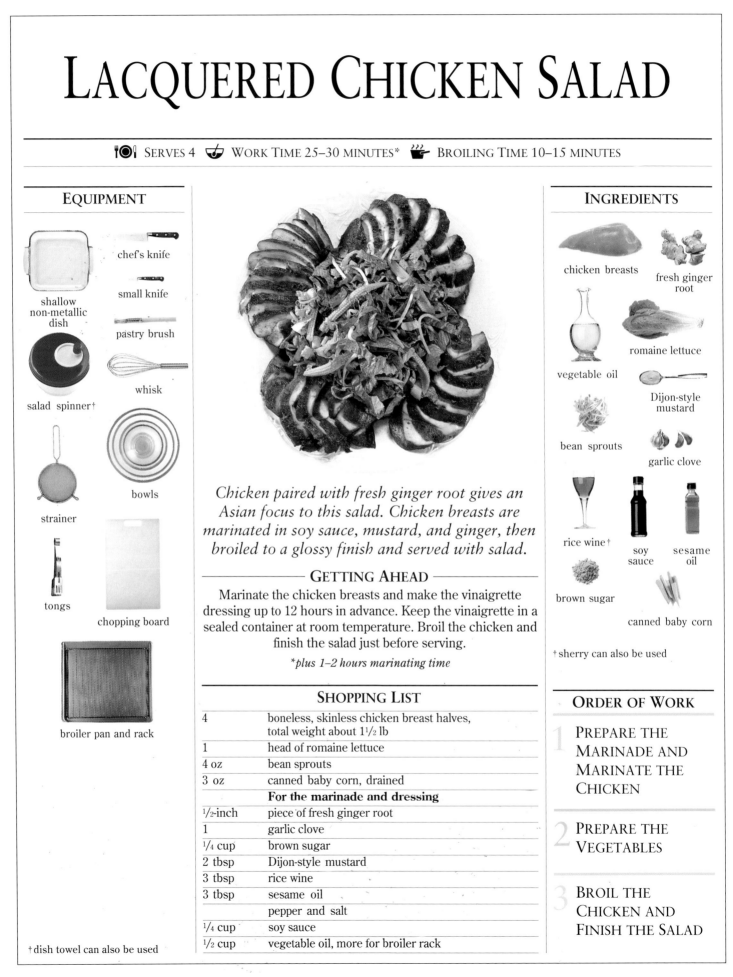

*Chicken paired with fresh ginger root gives an
Asian focus to this salad. Chicken breasts are
marinated in soy sauce, mustard, and ginger, then
broiled to a glossy finish and served with salad.*

GETTING AHEAD
Marinate the chicken breasts and make the vinaigrette
dressing up to 12 hours in advance. Keep the vinaigrette in a
sealed container at room temperature. Broil the chicken and
finish the salad just before serving.

*plus 1–2 hours marinating time

INGREDIENTS

chicken breasts

fresh ginger
root

vegetable oil

romaine lettuce

Dijon-style
mustard

bean sprouts

garlic clove

rice wine †

soy
sauce

sesame
oil

brown sugar

canned baby corn

† sherry can also be used

SHOPPING LIST

4	boneless, skinless chicken breast halves, total weight about 1½ lb
1	head of romaine lettuce
4 oz	bean sprouts
3 oz	canned baby corn, drained
	For the marinade and dressing
½-inch	piece of fresh ginger root
1	garlic clove
¼ cup	brown sugar
2 tbsp	Dijon-style mustard
3 tbsp	rice wine
3 tbsp	sesame oil
	pepper and salt
¼ cup	soy sauce
½ cup	vegetable oil, more for broiler rack

ORDER OF WORK

**1 PREPARE THE
MARINADE AND
MARINATE THE
CHICKEN**

**2 PREPARE THE
VEGETABLES**

**3 BROIL THE
CHICKEN AND
FINISH THE SALAD**

1 PREPARE THE MARINADE AND MARINATE THE CHICKEN

Remove tough tendons before cooking chicken breast

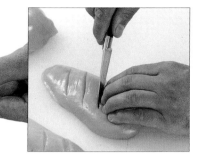

1 Strip the tendon from the underside of each chicken breast, stroking it with the small knife to remove it cleanly. Lightly score the top of each chicken breast. Set in the dish.

2 Peel and chop the fresh ginger root (see box, below). Set the flat side of the chef's knife on top of the garlic clove and strike it with your fist. Discard the skin and chop the garlic.

4 Pour the marinade over the chicken, cover, and refrigerate, 1–2 hours; turn breasts 3–4 times.

3 For the marinade, combine the ginger, garlic, brown sugar, mustard, 1 tbsp each of the rice wine and sesame oil, and pepper in a bowl. Pour in the soy sauce and stir to mix. Pour 1/4 cup of the marinade into another bowl and reserve.

5 For the dressing, add the remaining rice wine and sesame oil to the reserved marinade, and whisk to mix. Gradually whisk in the vegetable oil, so the dressing emulsifies and thickens slightly. Taste for seasoning and set aside.

HOW TO PEEL AND CHOP FRESH GINGER ROOT

3 Finely chop the slices of ginger root, using your knuckles to guide the blade.

1 With a small knife, peel the skin from the ginger root. Slice the ginger root with a chef's knife, cutting across the fibrous grain.

2 Place the chef's knife flat on each slice of ginger root and crush with the side or heel of your hand.

Tuck fingers under while chopping

2 PREPARE THE VEGETABLES

Stack and roll up
leaves for speedy
shredding

2 Pick over the bean sprouts and put them in a bowl. Cover them generously with boiling water and let stand, 1 minute. Drain, rinse with cold, running water, and drain again.

Shredded lettuce is
easy to mix with other
ingredients

1 Twist off and discard the root end from the romaine lettuce. Wash the leaves in plenty of cold water, then rinse individual leaves under cold, running water. Discard the tough stems. Dry the leaves in the salad spinner. Stack 5–6 of the leaves, roll them up tightly, and shred them. Repeat with the remaining leaves, and put them in a large bowl.

3 With the chef's knife, cut each of the ears of baby corn lengthwise in half. Set them aside.

3 BROIL THE CHICKEN AND FINISH THE SALAD

1 Heat the broiler and oil the broiler rack. Transfer the breasts from the marinade to the rack, and brush them with the marinade. Broil the chicken breasts about 3 inches from the heat, brushing often with marinade until they are well browned, 5–7 minutes.

Brush chicken often
with marinade during
broiling to give
lacquered look

2 Turn the breasts over. Brush them with more marinade. Broil until they are well browned, glossy, and tender, a further 5–7 minutes.

3 Meanwhile, add the bean sprouts and baby corn to the lettuce. Briskly whisk the dressing again to re-emulsify it.

4 Pour the dressing over the salad. Toss the salad and taste for seasoning. Arrange it in the center of a serving plate.

5 When the chicken breasts are cooked and well glazed, put them on the chopping board and cut each one diagonally into slices.

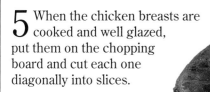

Cut chicken breasts diagonally for generous slices

¶⊙¶ TO SERVE
Fan the chicken slices in 4 sections around the salad, and serve while still hot.

Bean sprouts
add Asian touch to salad

Tangy marinade
broils to brilliant lacquered finish

VARIATION
TERIYAKI CHICKEN SALAD
In this simple variation of Lacquered Chicken Salad, the marinade has a more pronounced flavor typical of Japanese teriyaki.

1 Omit the brown sugar and mustard. Make the marinade as directed, using ¹/₂ cup light soy sauce and adding 2 tbsp granulated sugar and 2 tbsp of the vegetable oil.
2 Transfer ¹/₄ cup of the marinade mixture to another bowl, add the remaining rice wine and sesame oil, and whisk to mix. Gradually whisk in the remaining vegetable oil, so the dressing emulsifies and thickens slightly. Taste, season, and set aside.
3 Omit the baby corn. Cut around the core of 1 red bell pepper. Twist, pull out, and discard the core. Halve the pepper and scrape out the seeds. Cut away the white ribs on the inside. Set each half cut-side down, flatten it with the heel of your hand, and slice it lengthwise into thin strips. Put the strips in the bowl with the dressing; leave to soften, 1–2 hours. Marinate the chicken breasts as directed.
4 Meanwhile, prepare the lettuce and bean sprouts as directed. Broil the chicken breasts, let them cool, then cut into thin diagonal slices.
5 Put the lettuce and bean sprouts in a large bowl. Add the bell pepper strips with the dressing, and toss to mix. Taste the salad for seasoning, and transfer it to 4 individual plates. Arrange the chicken slices to the side.

THANKSGIVING WILD RICE SALAD

🍽 SERVES 8   🥄 WORK TIME 30–35 MINUTES*   🍲 COOKING TIME ¾–1¼ HOURS

EQUIPMENT

- bowls
- slotted spoon
- whisk
- chef's knife
- small knife
- vegetable peeler
- colander
- wooden spoon
- citrus juicer
- large metal spoon
- strainer
- shallow baking dish
- saucepans, 1 with lid
- baking sheet
- chopping board

Wild rice is tossed with pecans, orange zest, and cranberry dressing and topped with sliced smoked turkey breast. This salad tastes even better after standing a few hours, and is an ideal dish for holiday buffets.

GETTING AHEAD

You can prepare the wild rice salad up to 1 day ahead. Keep it, covered, in the refrigerator. Let the salad come to room temperature before serving.

*plus at least 1 hour standing time

SHOPPING LIST

6 cups	water
	salt and pepper
2 cups	wild rice
½ cup	pecans
¾ lb	sliced smoked turkey breast
	For the cranberry dressing
1½ cups	fresh cranberries
¼ cup	sugar
1	orange
2	shallots
¼ cup	cider vinegar
½ cup	safflower oil

INGREDIENTS

- smoked turkey breast
- fresh cranberries †
- pecans
- wild rice
- cider vinegar
- sugar
- orange
- safflower oil ‡
- shallots

† defrosted cranberries can also be used

‡ light vegetable oil can also be used

ANNE SAYS

"If fresh or frozen cranberries are unavailable, use ½ lb dried cranberries. Omit the step of cooking them."

ORDER OF WORK

1 PREPARE THE RICE, CRANBERRIES, AND PECANS

2 PREPARE THE ZEST, DRESSING, AND TURKEY; ASSEMBLE THE SALAD

PREPARE THE RICE, CRANBERRIES, AND PECANS

1 Put the water in a large saucepan with 1 tsp salt and bring to a boil. Stir in the rice, cover, and simmer until tender, about 1 hour. Meanwhile, prepare the cranberries and pecans.

ANNE SAYS
"Some types of wild rice take longer to cook than others, so follow package directions when preparing wild rice."

2 Heat the oven to 375°F. Spread the cranberries in the baking dish, sprinkle with sugar, and bake in the heated oven until they start to pop, 10–15 minutes for fresh, 5–8 minutes for defrosted cranberries. Let cool in the dish.

Sprinkle sugar evenly over cranberries

Cooked grains of wild rice burst open

HOW TO TOAST PECANS

Heat the oven to 350°F. Spread the pecans on a baking sheet and bake them in the heated oven until crisp, stirring occasionally so they toast evenly, 5–8 minutes.

Oven toasting brings out rich flavor of pecans

Pecans are crisped by toasting

3 Toast the pecans (see box, left). Coarsely chop the nuts. Use the colander to drain any excess water from the rice. Let cool. Transfer the cooled rice to a large bowl. Set aside.

2 PREPARE THE ZEST, DRESSING, AND TURKEY; ASSEMBLE THE SALAD

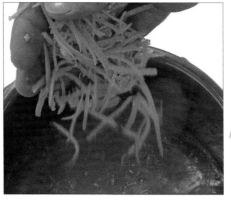

3 With the chef's knife, finely chop the orange julienne, and set aside.

1 Using the vegetable peeler, pare the zest from the orange, leaving behind the white pith. Cut the orange zest into very fine julienne strips.

2 Bring a small saucepan of water to a boil, and add the orange julienne. Simmer 2 minutes, then drain.

Gather strips together so they are easy to chop

4 Squeeze the juice from the orange. There should be about ⅓ cup. Pour the orange juice into a bowl.

Orange juice adds special character to dressing

5 Peel the shallots; separate into sections, if necessary. Hold 1 shallot or section steady with your fingers and slice horizontally toward the root, leaving the slices attached at the root. Slice vertically, almost to the root, and cut across to make fine dice. Continue chopping until very fine. Repeat with the remaining shallot.

6 Add the vinegar, diced shallots, salt, and pepper to the orange juice. Gradually whisk in the oil so the dressing emulsifies and thickens slightly. Taste for seasoning.

7 With a slotted spoon, transfer the cooled cranberries from the baking dish to the bowl of dressing, leaving the cranberry juice behind. Stir well to mix.

Peel shallot using small knife

Root end holds shallot together for chopping

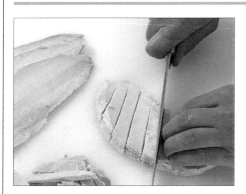

8 If necessary, remove the skin from the smoked turkey breast. Stack 2–3 slices on the chopping board, and cut them into ½-inch diagonal strips. Repeat with the remaining turkey.

ANNE SAYS

"Diagonal strips of turkey give the most attractive presentation."

9 Add the chopped pecans, orange zest, and two-thirds of the cranberry dressing to the wild rice. Toss until well combined. Let stand, 1 hour. Taste for seasoning.

Spoon cranberries carefully so they hold their shape

Smoked turkey breast is great holiday ingredient

¶◎¶   TO SERVE
Transfer the wild rice salad to a serving platter and arrange the turkey strips over the center. Spoon the remaining cranberry dressing on top of the turkey strips.

Cranberries give festive accent

VARIATION

WILD RICE SALAD WITH SMOKED DUCK BREAST

Smoked duck breast replaces the turkey breast in this elegant salad. If duck is not available, you can use smoked ham or chicken breast.

1 Omit the cranberries, sugar, orange, and smoked turkey breast. Cook the wild rice as directed. Chop the shallots as directed. Coarsely chop the leaves from 6–8 sprigs of parsley.
2 With a small knife, trim the stems from ½ lb fresh wild mushrooms, such as oyster or shiitake mushrooms, and wipe them with damp paper towels. Thinly slice them.
3 Heat 1 tbsp vegetable oil in a frying pan, and sauté the shallots, stirring occasionally, about 1 minute.
4 Add the sliced mushrooms with salt and pepper, and cook until all the liquid has evaporated, 3–5 minutes. Transfer the mixture to the wild rice.
5 Toast ¾ cup walnut halves as for the pecans. Set 8 aside, then coarsely chop the rest. Whisk ¼ cup cider vinegar with salt and pepper. Gradually whisk in ⅔ cup walnut oil.
6 Cut 2 smoked duck breasts (total weight about ¾ lb) into thin slices.
7 Pour the dressing over the rice and vegetables, add the chopped parsley and walnuts, and toss thoroughly. Arrange the salad on individual plates. Top with the smoked duck breast slices, and a walnut half.

SALADS KNOW-HOW

Each salad invites the addition of a personal touch. The recipe may list ingredients, dressings, and ideas for presentation, but the way is always open for you to use your own creative ideas for seasonal vegetables or fruit, or specialty seasonings. The position of salad in a meal is also your choice, be it appetizer, main course, or accompaniment. Salad may also make an appearance after the main course to refresh the palate before dessert, or to act as a light accompaniment to a cheese course.

CHOOSING SALADS

There are salads to suit every menu and, in this book, every place in the meal except dessert. If you have a garden, you are especially fortunate because a salad of freshly picked greens, tossed with a simple oil and vinegar dressing, is unbeatable. When choosing a recipe, take advantage of the seasons, serving vegetables that are at their peak of both freshness and flavor. Tender young spinach and asparagus herald the spring, featuring in salads with hot bacon dressing or vinaigrette. In the summer months, choose salads that highlight vine-ripened tomatoes or melons. Wonderful fall salads can be made with fennel bulb and pears, or with salmon and lamb's lettuce, while in cold weather, a warming salad based on lentils and sausage is very welcome.

SALADS AND YOUR HEALTH

A well-chosen salad, with a balance of ingredients united by an appropriate dressing, is the healthiest of foods. So many common salad ingredients – lettuce, tomatoes, bell peppers, and cabbage to name just a few – contain no fat or cholesterol, and are low in carbohydrates and sodium. But do not think that all foods in the guise of a salad are without reproach. If you are especially concerned about fat and calories, here are some points to consider when preparing salads. Begin with those that have little added fat, such as Greek Salad or Leeks Vinaigrette. Salade Niçoise, Tropical Chicken Salad, and Middle Eastern Salads are also good choices, with plenty of protein and mainly low-fat ingredients. Avoid salads with high-calorie ingredients, such as avocado or bacon; omit nuts and high-fat cheeses where possible. Replace mayonnaise or sour cream with non-fat yogurt.

STORING SALADS

The key to a salad's excellence is freshness, and often it must be finished and tossed in a vinaigrette or other dressing just before serving to achieve this. However, most ingredients can be prepared ahead: lettuce and other salad greens can be trimmed, washed, and stored in the refrigerator for up to a day, loosely wrapped in a damp dish towel. Toss the greens with dressing just prior to serving because the acid of vinegar or lemon juice will wilt the leaves.

Root vegetables, such as carrots and potatoes, and robust greens, such as cabbage, are more hardy. They can be prepared, dressed, and kept for a day or more in the refrigerator. Note that potatoes must be tossed with dressing while still warm to prevent discoloration while being chilled in the refrigerator. In fact, any salad with roots or grains is best made in advance so the flavors develop and mellow on standing. As an added convenience, such salads seldom require elaborate presentation, and are often served family-style straight from the bowl. Coleslaw, Black Forest Potato Salad, and the bulghur wheat and couscous salads that form part of Middle Eastern Salads and Mediterranean Salads are typical examples, and are ideal for casual, outdoor meals, such as barbecues or picnics. When you are looking at an individual recipe, be sure to read the section on Getting Ahead, so that you can fit the preparation plan it describes into your schedule.

MICROWAVE COOKING

You can blanch or pre-cook vegetables, such as carrots, green beans, or cauliflower, in the microwave. Chicken breasts in Waldorf Chicken Salad can be poached in the microwave, as can the knackwurst for the lentil salad.

You can peel the skin from onions, garlic, and tomatoes: heat onions and garlic cloves at High (100% power) just until warm, about 1 minute for onions, and 20–30 seconds for garlic; put tomatoes in boiling water in a microwave-safe container and cook until the skin splits, about 45 seconds. You can also toast nuts and cook bacon in the microwave.

SERVING SALADS

A salad, with its colorful, leafy components, appeals as much to the eye as the taste. Fresh herbs, thinly pared peel of vegetables featuring in the salad itself, blanched citrus zest, or strips of toasted tortilla are appealing toppings. Other traditional salad garnishes include fried croûtons, hard-boiled egg, tomato or radish roses, and grated or shaved Parmesan cheese. A sprinkling of fresh berries or toasted nuts adds character, with edible flowers perhaps the most whimsical ornament of all. Remember, however, that a salad decoration should reflect the flavors of the salad itself – chopped hazelnuts, for example, should indicate a salad dressed with hazelnut oil, and not be added arbitrarily.

Salads are called "composed" when the ingredients are arranged on individual plates to achieve an eye-catching presentation, with a pleasing contrast of color. These salads – Avocado and Grapefruit Salad and Fantasia Salad with Cheese Wafers are examples – require a little extra time to arrange, but the results are well worth it. More rustic salads invite a less formal presentation. They are tossed, then served directly from the salad bowl at the table.

SALAD DRESSINGS

Dressing plays a definitive role in any salad, and this book covers a wide range of dressings, from light or tart to rich, creamy, or full-bodied. Basic vinaigrette dressing is used most frequently, combining vinegar (or another acid, such as lemon juice) with salt, pepper, and often mustard or another piquant seasoning. Then oil is whisked in to emulsify the dressing.

The oil used can be peanut or corn (agreeably light); olive (rich and unmistakable in flavor – extra-virgin is the best); walnut or hazelnut (distinctly nutty); or nearly flavorless safflower or sunflower oil. If you like, oils such as safflower and hazelnut can be mixed together to achieve a moderate balance.

The vinegar used in vinaigrette dressing can be made from red or white wine, sherry, or even Champagne, for an especially delicate flavor. Balsamic vinegar is an Italian inspiration of sweet wine long aged in wooden casks, giving a characteristic robust, fruity flavor. Other vinegars used in salads include cider (with a subtle hint of apple), rice wine (for an Asian touch), and flavored wine vinegars, such as berry or herb. Lemon juice, or other citrus juices, can replace the vinegar in a vinaigrette, but use only half the amount of vinegar called for in the recipe.

Possible additions to a salad dressing include chopped herbs, garlic, shallots, horseradish, cheese, berry purée, chopped nuts, honey, or poppy seeds. Some dressings are based on marinade ingredients, such as soy sauce,

HOW-TO BOXES

In each of the recipes in **Superb Salads,** *you will find pictures of all the techniques used. However, some basic preparations appear in a number of recipes and these are shown in extra detail in these special "how-to" boxes:*

Worcestershire sauce, fresh ginger root, or capers. Apart from vinaigrette dressings, you can also learn in this volume how to dress salads with mayonnaise, yogurt, sour cream, buttermilk, and even spicy peanut sauce. When choosing a dressing, always have the ingredients of your salad in mind. Mild, tender greens, such as leaf lettuce, Belgian endive, and lamb's lettuce deserve a delicate vinaigrette of red or white wine vinegar and light peanut or olive oil. More assertive greens, such as spinach or curly endive, can stand up to a vinaigrette with balsamic vinegar or hazelnut oil. And heavier, starchy foods, such as lentils or dried beans, can take the most spirited dressings, with a backing of garlic or fresh hot chili peppers.

FLAVORED OILS

Oils that have been infused with herbs or spices are ideal for seasoning salad dressings and marinades rather than for cooking. Their flavors are often so strong that just a few drops will pervade a whole dish. Popular herbs for making infused oils are tarragon, basil, mint, marjoram, thyme, rosemary, and savory, while garlic and hot chili peppers are also common flavorings. For stronger flavored oil, discard and replace the herbs after 1 week. Also, the longer you leave the oil to infuse, the stronger the flavor will be.

HERB OIL

🍴 MAKES 3 CUPS OIL

🥣 WORK TIME 5–10 MINUTES

🍲 INFUSING TIME 1–2 WEEKS

SHOPPING LIST

1	bunch of fresh basil or tarragon, or 5–7 sprigs of fresh rosemary or thyme, or any combination of herbs
3 cups	extra-virgin olive oil

1 Lay the herbs on a chopping board and bruise them by pounding 5–6 times with a rolling pin to help draw out their flavor. Put the herbs in a 3-cup glass jar or bottle.

2 Pour the oil over the herbs, seal the jar or bottle, and leave to infuse in a cool place before using, 1–2 weeks.

VARIATIONS

HOT CHILI-PEPPER OIL

1 Split 2–3 fresh or dried hot chili peppers, discarding the seeds if you would like a less fiery flavor. Put the chili peppers in a 3-cup glass jar or bottle. Pour the oil over the chili peppers, seal the jar or bottle, and leave to infuse in a cool place before using, 1–2 weeks.

GARLIC OIL

1 Peel 4–5 garlic cloves: set the flat side of a chef's knife on top of each garlic clove, strike it with your fist, and discard the skin. Put the garlic in a 3-cup glass jar or bottle. Pour the oil over the garlic, seal the jar or bottle, and leave to infuse in a cool place before using, 1–2 weeks.

FLAVORED VINEGARS

A variety of flavored vinegars is available, but you can just as easily create them at home at low cost. Use flavored vinegars in salads, marinades, and other preparations. Herbs, especially tarragon, are the most common flavoring, but garlic or berry vinegars are also delicious.

Vinegars must be stored in a sterilized jar or bottle to ensure they do not spoil. To sterilize a heatproof jar or bottle: put the container on its side in a saucepan of boiling water. Boil 10 minutes, then let the container cool slightly in the water. Drain it and leave to steam dry in a low oven.

HERB VINEGAR

🍴 MAKES 3 cups VINEGAR

🥣 WORK TIME 10–15 MINUTES

🍲 INFUSING TIME 2 WEEKS

SHOPPING LIST

1	bunch of fresh tarragon or basil, or 5–7 sprigs of fresh rosemary or thyme, or any combination of herbs
3 cups	white wine vinegar

1 Lay the herbs on a chopping board and bruise them by pounding 5–6 times with a rolling pin to help draw out their flavor. Put the herbs in a 3-cup sterilized jar or bottle.

2 Bring the vinegar just to a boil and pour it over the flavoring. Let cool, seal the jar or bottle, and leave in a cool place to steep, at least 2 weeks, shaking it sometimes.

3 Strain the vinegar through cheesecloth or paper coffee filters into a newly sterilized glass jar or bottle. If you like, add fresh flavoring for an attractive presentation. Seal the jar or bottle, and store it in a cool, dry place.

VARIATIONS

GARLIC VINEGAR

1 Peel 4–5 garlic cloves. Put the garlic in a 3-cup sterilized glass jar or bottle, and finish as directed.

FRUIT VINEGAR

1 Pick over 1/2 lb fresh fruit, such as raspberries or blueberries, rinse with cold water, and drain. Put in a 3-cup sterilized glass jar or bottle, and finish as directed.

DECORATIONS FOR SALADS

*The presentation of a salad improves dramatically with an eye-catching decoration.
Here are just a few ideas for highlighting or complementing salad ingredients.*

APPLE CHEVRON

*Apple chevrons are easy
to cut but look spectacular as a
salad decoration.*

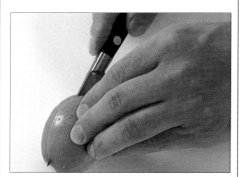

1 Cut an apple into 4 wedges.
  Remove the core from each wedge.
Starting at the outermost edge of a
wedge, cut a V-shaped slice in it.

2 Continue to
  cut V-shapes,
working inward until
there are 6 slices.
Fan them out slightly
and sprinkle cut
surfaces with lemon
juice so they do
not discolor.

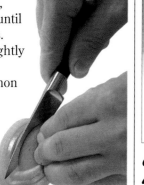

SALMON ROSE

*Roses of smoked salmon
strips are a delicate decoration,
delicious with fish salads.*

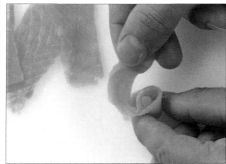

1 For a single salmon rose, cut
  5 salmon strips, about 1-inch wide.
Holding one end of a strip between the
thumb and forefinger of one hand,
guide the strip around with the fingers
of your other hand to form the center.

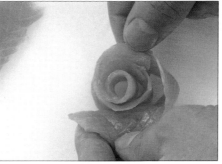

2 Shape the remaining strips loosely
  around the first to form the petals.
If you like, add a flat-leaf parsley sprig.

CITRUS CORONETS

*Citrus fruit cut into coronets are
a versatile decoration for a wide
range of dishes.*

Steady
fruit on
work
surface

1 Push tip of
  a small knife
straight through
center of fruit at a
sharp angle. Reinsert at
opposite angle to meet tip of first cut.

2 Continue around fruit in a zigzag
  pattern. Twist and pull halves apart.
Trim ends so coronets sit flat.

INDEX

ACKNOWLEDGMENTS

*Photographer*s David Murray
Jules Selmes
Photographer's Assistant Ian Boddy

Chef Eric Treuille
Cookery Consultant Martha Holmberg
Home Economist Sarah Lowman

US Editor Jeanette Mall

Typesetting Linda Parker
Text film by Disc to Print (UK) Limited

Production Consultant Lorraine Baird

*Anne Willan would like to thank
her chief editor Cynthia Nims and
associate editor Jacqueline Bobrow for
their vital help with writing this book
and researching and testing the recipes,
aided by Alexandra Guarnaschelli,
Jane Reilly, and La Varenne's chefs
and trainees.*